The COMPLETE MANUAL OF *Sewing*

120 Visual Lessons for Beginners

stashBOOKS®

an imprint of C&T Publishing

CONTENTS

The Complete Manual of Sewing

PART I

GETTING EQUIPPED

GOOD TOOLS MAKE GOOD WORKERS.

ORGANIZING

YOUR WORK SPACE

SEWING TAKES TIME AND SPACE AND IS RARELY FINISHED IN ONE SESSION. IN ORDER TO SAVE TIME AND BE EFFICIENT, IT IS IMPORTANT TO SET UP A DEDICATED SEWING STATION.

SET UP

Having a dedicated sewing area is ideal, whether it's a separate room— the best option—or a table in the corner of your living room. This is handy in case you need to leave your project and come back to it later without constantly moving your sewing supplies back and forth. Use a table that is large enough to cut fabric easily. It should be at least 40˝ (1.1 m). Make sure you have enough light by sewing near a window or having a good lamp.

FABRICS

Over time, you will build up an excellent fabric collection. Wash new fabrics as soon as you buy them, so they are ready to use as soon as a new project comes up. Store your fabrics rolled instead of folden on shelves. The fabrics will take up less space and will be easier to grab. If you are super organized, you can label them with the fabric type and length. Remember to store your fabrics away from direct sunlight as the colors will fade quickly.

PATTERNS

Create a storage system for your patterns. Stack them on a shelf so they're within easy reach, or put them in plastic boxes to keep them from collecting dust.

TOOLS AND NOTIONS

All of your sewing tools and notions should be easily accessible. Store them in separate boxes. Put your marking and cutting tools in a dedicated drawer or small container. Also, provide storage for your threads and bobbins.

Some Rules to Keep in Mind

Set up a large enough table to work comfortably at with all your materials.

Make sure you have good lighting.

Read the instructions in full before you start and follow the recommended order.

Remember to wash your hands regularly to avoid soiling the thread or fabric.

In sewing, as in all crafts, mastery comes with experience. To sew well, take the time to practice. Avoid setting the bar too high. Start with simple sewing patterns. If you are only comfortable with straight stitching, start with projects that can be made using the straight stitch.

GETTING

THE RIGHT EQUIPMENT

BEFORE YOU GET STARTED, YOU NEED TO MAKE SURE YOU HAVE THE RIGHT TOOLS. SOME TOOLS ARE CRUCIAL, WHILE THE OTHERS ARE HANDY TO HAVE, IF NEEDED. YOU CAN EASILY FIND THESE IN SEWING AND CRAFT STORES OR ON THE INTERNET.

MEASURING TOOLS

To ensure that a piece of clothing fits correctly, it is essential to measure and take dimensions with quality tools. This will help you know what to cut and how much fabric is needed. There are several tools for different purposes.

▸ **A 20″ (50cm) or longer flat ruler:** To draw straight lines when copying a pattern.

▸ **A 90° ruler:** To make sure you can draw right angles.

▸ **A tape measure:** A tape measure is used to measure a pattern's curves and take measurements. The standard length is at least 60″ (150cm) long. If you are working with significant amounts of fabric, use a longer tape measure. If possible, buy one with the same width as the standard seam allowance. Choose a plastic tape measure because it keeps its shape.

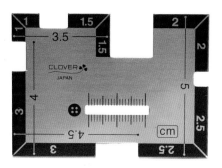

▸ **Sewing gauge:** This small metal or plastic ruler has **standard graduations:** ¼″, ⅜″, ½″, ⅝″, ¾″, 1″, 1⅛″, 1¼″, 1⅜″. It is convenient for measuring, transferring small dimensions, and hemming. Some are heat-resistant and can be ironed.

▸ **Sewing gauge with sliding marker:** This small ruler has a window in the center to move a sliding marker, which can shift to a precise measurement. It helps mark seam allowances and hems, but you can also use it to mark the position of buttons, clips, and more.

▸ **Quilting ruler:** This transparent ruler is squared vertically and horizontally. It has grid lines that make it helpful to add seam allowances, draw hems, or check right angles. It is widely used for patchwork.

▸ **The curved ruler or French curve:** A French curve is a curved ruler that imitates the body's curves and is used to draw or modify patterns.

MARKING TOOLS

Whether you are sewing by hand or stitching with a machine, you can use different tools to mark on both paper and fabric.

ON PAPER

It is customary in sewing to not cut the pattern, but to trace it on another piece of paper. This keeps the original pattern intact. To do this you will need a pencil, an eraser, and pattern paper.

THERE ARE SEVERAL TYPES OF PATTERN MATERIAL.

Choose your preferred material according to your needs:

▸ **Tissue paper** is very fragile. One side is smooth and shiny, and the other is matte. The smooth side is placed on the pattern.

▸ **Pattern paper** simplifies copying, but may tear easily when it is handled.

▸ **Lightweight white kraft paper** is a good compromise between transparency and strength.

▸ **Template plastic** is solid, but difficult to cut and does not show well on fabrics when cutting.

▸ **Swedish tracing paper** (which is not Swedish) is a soft and translucent paper that is more robust than tissue paper. This paper is flexible enough to be "molded" around the body, allowing you to make adjustments and avoid stiff muslins.

▸ **Carbon paper** is covered with colored wax on one side, it is placed between the fabric and the pattern with the wax side facing the fabric. Use a tracing wheel to transfer the pattern lines. There are several colors of carbon paper available. Choose the color that works best for your fabric.

■ TYPES OF PAPER FOR TRACING PATTERNS

MATERIAL TYPE	TRANSPARENCY	STRENGTH	STORAGE
Tissue paper	Very good	Very fragile	Easy to fold; not very bulky
Pattern paper	Good	Fragile	Fairly stiff folds; quite bulky
Lightweight kraft paper	Fair	Strong	Quite bulky
Template plastic	Very good	Strong	Quite bulky
Swedish tracing paper	Good	Fairly strong	Quite bulky
Carbon paper	Not transparent	Strong	Easy to fold

CUTTING TOOLS

Once the pattern has been copied onto the paper, it may be traced onto the fabric with all the marks. You can choose between several tools for this:

▸ **Tailor's chalk:** This is the traditional material for marking fabric. It comes in various colors—yellow or white for dark fabrics, red or blue for light fabrics—and multiple shapes. Trim the edges or tip of the chalk well.

▸ **Powdered chalk:** This is a small box or pen containing white or colored powdered chalk. Place the applicator on the desired spot, and the powder will come out. This allows you to make fine, precise lines.

▸ **Chalk pencils:** These mark the fabric like tailor's chalk and powdered chalk but don't need sharpening.

▸ **Water-, air-, and heat- erasable fabric pens:** It is best to test these pens on a piece of cloth to ensure that the ink is sufficiently visible and, above all, that it erases well, some pens disappear under heat, some when washed.

▸ **A tracing wheel** is used with carbon paper. There are two types: The "smooth" pattern roller allows you to trace continuously, while the "notched" roller allows you to trace in the form of marking points.

▸ You can also use a **small piece of dry soap.** It marks perfectly on the fabric.

Sewing often involves cutting paper, fabrics, and threads. This means that you need several pairs of scissors just for sewing.

▸ **Paper scissors:** These are essential for cutting patterns. Using fabric scissors on paper causes micro-abrasions on the blades, invisible to the naked eye, that damage your fabrics when you cut them.

▸ **Fabric scissors:** Sometimes called tailor's scissors, shears, or sewing scissors, these are one of the most important tools in your sewing kit! The main thing to remember is to use your fabric-cutting scissors only for that activity. Equipped with pointed tips, they should be long enough to have a good range and cut accurately and cleanly—usually between 8″ and 10″ (20 and 25cm) for adults. The longer the blades, the heavier the scissors. So, it's best to find the right compromise between size and weight. Note that if you regularly cut thick fabrics (denim, wool, and more), you may want to consider larger scissors 10″ to 11″ (25 to 27cm).

In terms of materials, we advise you to use stainless steel for durability.

Scissors must also fit your hand: You can try on scissors, just like gloves! You need to be comfortable when cutting and your scissors should allow you to have a good grip for precise cutting. Therefore, choose ergonomic handles, and be aware that right-handed and left-handed scissors are available.

Don't hesitate to invest in a pair of good scissors: They will last for years if they're maintained. And above all, put them in a safe place to prevent them from falling or being used for another purpose.

LOOKING AFTER YOUR SCISSORS

▶ **Essential maintenance advice includes giving your scissors a specific role:** This is the basic rule to ensure their usefulness over time. Beyond that, they require some regular maintenance. First, regularly wipe the blades with a soft cloth to remove dust and cutting residue that will inevitably accumulate, opening the blades as wide as possible to reach the smallest nooks and crannies. You can invest in a sharpener, available in some craft stores, to keep them sharp.

You can also use a piece of aluminum foil to sharpen the blades. Fold the foil into quarters and cut it into strips using the entire length of the blades. Then wipe your scissors with a soft cloth soaked in warm water. This does not prevent you from calling in a professional from time to time to sharpen your scissors. You can ask your local craft or fabric store, which likely has its scissors professionally sharpened.

Finally, as soon as you feel that the scissors are sticking a little when you cut, put a small drop of machine oil on the central screw to lubricate the base of the blades. Then wipe your scissors with a soft cloth to remove any oil residue that might stain your fabrics.

▶ **Embroidery scissors:** These small 3½″ to 4½″ (9 to 11cm) sharp scissors have a fine and very pointed blade for cutting threads or making notches in your fabric.

▶ **A thread cutter:** As the name suggests, it is used to cut thread quickly and precisely.

▶ **A seam ripper:** This is so essential—even for experienced sewists—that it is often included in the basic accessories supplied with a sewing machine. As the name suggests, it is used to quickly unstitch mistakes thanks to its small, sharp point, which is slipped under the thread of the seam to be removed and cut by pulling upwards. It is a much more precise tool than the tip of a scissor because it is much smaller. Don't be fooled, however: It requires meticulousness and precision to use—so don't go too fast—because while it cuts threads very well, it can also cut the fabric very well. Therefore, you must take your time—even if you rename it "slow seam ripper"—and make sure you only take the thread to be cut, not a thread from the fabric. It is also used to open buttonholes. You cannot sharpen this tool. When it becomes dull, throw it away!

OTHER CUTTING TOOLS

• ROTARY CUTTER

It can save time for simple cuts (squares or rectangles). The rotary cutter is less precise and flexible than scissors for curved shapes. It also requires a self-healing cutting mat and an acrylic or metal ruler. Perfectly suited to quilting, this tool can also be considered an accessory for garment sewing.

• PINKING SHEARS

Their saw-toothed blades allow them to notch fabric. They reduce the risk of fraying.

SEWING NOTIONS

NEEDLES

Despite their small size, needles are a very important part of sewing. They are chosen to match the fabric and thread used. The lighter and finer the fabric, the finer the needle must be to avoid breaking the fibers. There are two main categories of needles:

HAND SEWING NEEDLES

There are several types of needles for hand sewing. A number indicates their size: The larger the number, the finer and smaller the needle.

▸ **Sharps (or general purpose needles):** These are the most common needles. They have a round eye, a pointed tip, and are of medium length. They come in all sizes (sizes 1 to 12). Sizes 7 and 8 are the most common and useful. Buy sets of needles containing several sizes.

▸ **Milliners needles:** These are very long needles with a round eye. They are ideal for basting, gathering, and overcasting. They are available in sizes 3 to 12.

▸ **Ballpoint needles:** These needles are used to sew knits by hand. They are available in sizes 5 to 10.

▸ **Quilting needles:** These are shorter and thinner with a round eye. They are perfect for quilting and patchwork. You can also use them on thick fabrics such as jeans, denim, or tweed. They come in all sizes.

▸ **The thimble** protects your sewing finger from the point of the needle. It may be essential for hand sewing thick fabrics.

There are no hard-and-fast rules when choosing needles. Experience will tell you which ones to use, but always keep in mind that the needle must be compatible with the thickness of the thread. A needle that is too large will leave a hole in the fabric, while a needle that is too fine will weaken your thread.

TRICK

If you are unsure of which needle to choose, pierce a scrap piece of fabric and pick the needle that leaves the smallest hole in the material.

MACHINE SEWING NEEDLES

There are different types of needles to sew all kinds of fabrics. It is wise to buy the recommended needles for your machine's brand and part number. The higher the needle number, the larger the needle.

Sewing machine needles get damaged quickly; change them regularly (see Needles, page 49).

PINS

There is a wide variety of pins. They must be high quality so they do not damage the fabric. Steel pins are ideal as they will not dull as quickly. We'll look at a few types:

▸ **Household pins** of medium size and thickness can be used for all types of sewing work.

▸ **Glass-head pins** are longer than household pins. They are easy to spot.

▸ **Extra-fine pins** will not damage even the most delicate fabrics. They can be used in place of basting and a sewing machine can stitch over them.

▸ **Flat-head pins** are used to help pin pattern pieces for cutting.

▸ **Quilting pins** are very long and are used for patchwork or quilting.

▸ **Safety pins** can be used to feed elastic through fabric channels.

▸ **Clips and masking tape** are excellent alternatives to pins when pins can damage the fabric you are working on (such as oilcloth or leather).

▸ **Pincushions and pinholders** allow you to store pins without damaging them.

THREADS

It is essential to choose a quality thread suitable for your intended use. Cheap threads break or fray quickly and do not last very long on the spool.

▸ **Cotton or polyester sewing threads:** Whether you are sewing by hand or machine, select your thread according to the texture of the fabric. Thick fabrics require a strong thread, while thin and fragile fabrics should be sewn with a fine thread. Be aware that the higher the number, the finer the thread. For a classic cotton project, choose a size 70 or 80 thread.

▸ **For hand sewing,** use cotton thread for cotton fabrics and polyester thread for synthetic fibers.

▸ **For machine sewing,** choose a polyester thread. It is strong, does not shrink, and is more durable than cotton. It is also essential to have the same type of thread (fiber content and size) in the bobbin and spool.

TIP

It is customary to use the same color thread as your fabric. If you don't have a matching color, however, choose a slightly darker shade than the fabric. Remember that most of the seams in your project will probably be invisible on the outside (only the topstitching, hems, or buttonhole seams will show on the front of your garment). We suggest you use a thread color that shows on the fabric for your first few projects. This will help you see what you're doing and, if necessary, reduce the risk of cutting the material if you have to use a seam ripper.

▸ **Basting thread:** is a colored thread (it must be seen on your work) thick enough to be used with a hand sewing needle with a relatively large eye. It breaks easily, as it is intended to be temporary.

▸ **Hand quilting thread** is used to stitch the layers of a quilt together. It is more resistant to breakage and rubbing than traditional thread, thicker, and should slide perfectly through the fabric without making knots.

▸ **Metallic thread** has a metallic look for shiny finishes (embroidery stitches or topstitching). It requires a topstitching needle to prevent fraying or breaking.

▸ **Wooly nylon thread,** made of polyester or polyamide, is an elastic thread with good recovery. It is ideal for elastic seams (lingerie, sportswear, or any stitching in knit fabrics). This thread is a classic size (80) used in bobbins.

CLOSURES

These are more or less easy to install and contribute to the success of your work. You will have to choose between materials, colors, sizes, and shapes according to your type of project.

FASTENERS

Simple fasteners such as hook and eye closures and snaps come in different sizes, shapes, and colors.

Hook and eye closures work well for skirt and trouser waistbands. Sew them tightly to the edge of the garment so the fastener is not visible. Snaps consist of two interlocking parts. The part with a point (male) is the first part you attach to the top of the piece you want to "snap." Choose snaps attached to tape for children's blouses, coats, or aprons. Sew the tape along the openings on each side of the garment using a zipper foot.

ELASTICS

Elastic is very practical and helps simplify the construction of clothes and accessories.

Elastic is an easy way to avoid using zippers or making buttonholes. On your waist, wrists, ankles, back, or head, elastic adds design interest by creating a puffed or bloused effect. Consider using elastic for children's clothing because elastic is very convenient for putting on or taking off clothes.

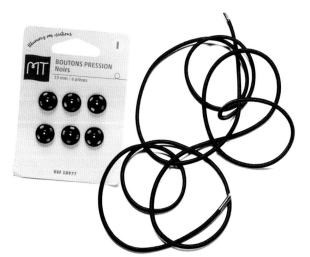

ELASTICS ARE AVAILABLE IN DIFFERENT WIDTHS, COLORS, AND SHAPES:

▸ **Knitted elastic:** The most classic elastic for waistbands, cuffs, ankles, hair bands, and pockets.

▸ **Elastic cord:** Secure hats under the chin, stitching gathers, or making jewelry.

▸ **Drawcord elastic:** To secure waistbands, used in conjunction with a drawstring.

▸ **Buttonhole elastic:** Very effective in adapting to multiple sizes, such as the tummies of expectant mothers.

BUTTONS

Buttons come in all shapes, sizes, and materials. They are usually sewn by hand. The number of buttons you use for a particular garment is not only a function of fashion, but also of practicality. Button and buttonhole locations are usually indicated on the pattern: Transfer them to your fabric. It is best to make the buttonholes before sewing on the buttons. This way, you can mark the location of the buttons with a pencil through the buttonholes. Buttonholes are usually placed ⅝″ (1.5cm) from the edge and at regular intervals from each other; they should be a little larger than the diameter of the buttons.

ZIPPERS

Invented in the early twentieth century (like pants for women), zippers were a small revolution in the clothing industry. Until then, opening and closing systems were buttons and cords!

Today, zippers are available in all types, sizes, and colors: invisible, separating, fancy, with double sliders, special ones for jeans, brass, metal, synthetic, and so on. They are mainly used in clothing for making pants, skirts, or jackets, but they are also used in home furnishings and leather goods to make cushion covers or bags.

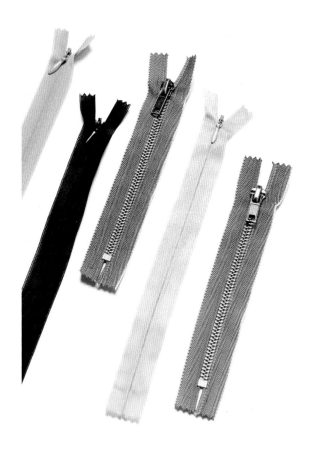

Ribbons and trim tend to look complicated, but they are straightforward to apply. They come in all shapes and styles and add a personal touch to your creations. Here are some of them, with their instructions for use.

RIBBONS AND TRIMS

Who hasn't felt inspired when looking at a display dripping with ribbons and trimmings of all types and colors? Do you always buy a few yards, but never really know how to use them? Here is a short explanlation of each type to help you understand their characteristics and uses.

‣ **Decorative ribbon:** Available in satin, muslin, cotton, linen, organza, imitation leather, plain or printed—and in all widths—decorative ribbon is often used in home decor or as a tie in garments. Slipped through a waistband or pocket channel with a safety pin, they can also be used as cords.

‣ **Fancy trim:** Fringed or feathered, with pompons, pearls, sequins, lace, or fur, or woven, braided, jacquard, or brocade, there is a trim for any look!

Sewn on the bottom of a skirt or on the cuffs of a jacket, they will add a touch of originality to your creations and freshness to your clothes.

‣ **Bias tape** (available in various materials, colors, and prints) is great for impeccable finishes and can be applied to both straight edges and curves. Bias tape is sewn on fabric edges, once on the wrong side and then folded to the right side and stitched in place.

‣ **Hook-and-loop tape** (available in all widths and colors) is very practical for making children's costumes or small pouches.

‣ **Grosgrain** is patterned or plain and available in several sizes. It is ideal for pretty neckline finishes or attaching waistbands of skirts and pants. It is also very effective for creating bag handles.

‣ **Piping:** Plain or decorative, piping slips between two layers of fabric to accentuate the seams in a cushion, a bag, or the outlines of a jacket.

‣ **Lace:** Often used in home decor, you can use it to embellish a garment or a hat.

‣ **Rickrack** adds a personal touch, hides a seam, or borders the bottom of a dress.

‣ **Cords—braided or rattail,** in cotton, leather, linen, suede, polyester, or elastic—are very popular in home furnishings and trimmings. They have practical uses in clothing construction, in making accessories, and in making ties.

SEW-ON BAG HANDLES

Usually added during the final steps of construction, bag handles are often made of leather or imitation leather. They are usually sewn by hand with a special needle for leather and are often pre-stitched with small holes that simplify the sewing. There are also fabric bag handles that can be machine stitched.

BUCKLES AND D-RINGS

Buckles and D-rings are made of metal or plastic and are used as closures for pockets and waistbands and as attachments for straps, tabs on the back of jackets, or bag handles. Some of these are sewn directly to your project the same way as bag handles. Others can be attached using ribbons or cords that you must sew onto your piece.

RIB TRIM

This knitted fabric is sold as a single ready made strip that can be used directly or by the yard to cut out yourself to use for collars, cuffs, and the waistbands of t-shirts, sweatshirts, shorts, and other garments. It is mainly used for finishing knitted fabrics. Ribbing comes in a multitude of colors to match fabrics easily. It is sewn with a ballpoint needle and an overlock or stretch machine stitch, giving your garments a ready-to-wear look.

SEW-ON COLLARS

For everything you create sewing and craft stores are full of embellishments such as pom-poms, balls, feathers, and embroidered or crocheted appliques that can be attached with just a few hand stitches!

▸ And for all your creations and customizations, sewing and crafting stores are full of small accessories such as pom-poms, balls, feathers, and embroidered or crocheted patterns to sew in a few strokes of the needle!

REINFORCING THE FABRIC

Lining, interfacing, fusible interfacing, and batting are the hidden heroes of sewing. Each can add body to a garment or decorative piece, add support and durability or make it warmer.

LINING

The lining covers the inside of a garment. It simplifies putting a garment on and makes it more comfortable to wear. Choose a good quality fabric, such as acetate or rayon. Remember that the lining should always be made of a lighter fabric than the garment. Choose a lining that has the same properties as the main fabric; it should be able to undergo the same cleaning treatment. Cut the lining from the same pattern pieces, following the same direction for the fabric whether straight or bias and transfer the markings, but plan for less length. Assemble it independently before attaching it to the main garment with the wrong side of the lining to the wrong side of the garment fabric.

INTERFACING

Interfacing is a piece of fabric that gives garments additional structure. It comes in different thicknesses and some can be ironed on. Interfacing that is not the iron-on type must be sewn onto the pattern pieces to attach it. Make sure to cut interfacing on the grain. Cut the interfacing to the size of each pattern piece and baste it to the wrong side of the main fabric.

Once assembled, the two fabrics are treated as one layer. The interfacing attaches to the entire work.

THERMAL-BONDING OR IRON-ON FUSIBLE INTERFACING

Fusible interfacing is a fabric that has glue applied to one side. The side with glue, which generally looks rough and shiny, is placed on the wrong side of the fabric.

Fusible interfacing stiffens a piece. It is applied to add a beautiful shape (collar, cutouts, and so on) or when the fabric will be cut and should be supported (buttonholes). There are several types of fusible interfacings. The nonwoven types come in several thicknesses and are applied independently of the grain. Woven fusible interfacing is also available in several thicknesses, but you must apply it with the grain. It is essential to adapt the interfacing to the primary material. For thin fabrics, choose interfacing on a knitted base; it will warp the fabric less. Use a cotton-based interfacing for thicker fabrics or if you need more reinforcement. Always test on a small piece of fabric before working on your project.

To apply, place the hot iron—without steam—on the back of the fabric, wait a few seconds, remove the iron, and then let the piece cool. To avoid gluing your board or iron, cut the pieces of fusible interfacing ³⁄₁₆″ (0.5cm) smaller around all edges.

STUFFING OR BATTING

Stuffing is generally synthetic, but can also be made from natural fibers (kapok). It is used to fill cushions and comforters. Batting comes in sheets sold by the meter and by the yard. Its composition can be organic or synthetic, and its thickness varies from thin to thick. It is used to make fleece fabrics (caught between two materials, stitched in a fine diamond pattern) and to fleece projects: game mats, tablet cases, and more.

Ironing TOOLS

WE CANNOT STRESS THE IMPORTANCE OF IRONING IN SEWING ENOUGH.

Get into the habit of taking out your ironing board as soon as you start a project. You must iron before tracing the pattern and cutting the fabric, and also during crucial stages of the sewing process (pressing the seams or marking the corners). You will need:

▸ **An iron.** Please don't skimp on quality, whether it's an iron or a steam iron. A quality iron will have a good steam flow and a slippery soleplate, and it will not drip or spit.

▸ **An ironing board.** The ideal ironing board will be adjustable in height and sufficiently long and wide. Choose a solid and stable model with a thick cotton cover.

▸ **A damp cloth.** This is a piece of cotton or white organza without seams. Wet it and place it between the fabric and the iron soleplate when ironing fragile fabrics.

▸ **A sleeve board.** This small wooden board wrapped in a cloth cover makes ironing cylindrical parts such as trouser legs, sleeves, and cuffs easier.

▸ **A tailor's ham.** This tightly stuffed pillow shape form has several curves tha simplify ironing darts, necklines, and curves. The ham helps keep the garment's shape and raises the part to be ironed, to avoid creasing the rest. You will find many online tutorials that show you how to make one yourself from fabric scraps.

‣ **Remove surface sizing** often present on purchased fabrics. Iron in the direction of the grain, with steady pressure, without lifting it from the fabric. Do not press too hard on the iron, as this may cause the fabric to stretch. Ironing allows the warp and weft threads to be straightened.

‣ **Remove creases.** Use steam if necessary. It can also help to spray a little water on stubborn wrinkles.

‣ **Pressing or opening seams with an iron:** As a last step after stitching press each seam with an iron before you sew the next one. Work from the wrong side and press the seam open with the tip of the iron, opening the seam allowances on each side. The idea is to press the iron (to lift and put it down) rather than slide it back and forth over the fabric.

Steam can help press the fabric well and gives clean edges.

For round seams or fabric fullness, press centimeter by centimeter or inch by inch so as not to crush the volume. Try rotating the fabric a little at a time around the end of the ironing board, working with a sleeve board, or better yet, a tailor's ham.

‣ **Thermal-bonding or iron-on fusible interfacing.** Place the fusible interfacing, adhesive side down, on the back of the fabric. Press without moving the iron for 10 seconds. Next move the iron by lifting it from the fabric and then press on the next section until all the fabric is fused with glue. Allow the fabric to cool before moving to avoid stretching or distorting the fabric.

‣ Choose the iron's temperature depending on the fabric type. Cotton and linens can be ironed at very hot temperatures. For woolens, very fine materials, and silk, lower the iron temperature, and consider ironing on the back of the fabric and using a damp cloth.

ABOUT

FABRICS

CHOOSE THE MOST SUITABLE FABRICS FOR YOUR PROJECTS TO GET THE BEST RESULTS. GO TO YOUR LOCAL FABRIC STORE WITH THE PATTERN YOU WANT TO MAKE. THE SALESPERSON MAY BE ABLE TO DIRECT YOU TO THE RIGHT FABRIC OR YOU WILL HAVE THINK ABOUT THE PATTERN SPECIFICATIONS AND FIND THE RIGHT MATCH YOURSELF.

Types OF FABRICS

BECAUSE OF THEIR DIFFERENT MANUFACTURING METHODS AND MATERIALS, NOT ALL FABRICS REACT THE SAME. THREE LEADING FAMILIES OF FABRICS ARE DETERMINED BY THE ORIGIN OF THE FIBERS WITH WHICH THEY ARE MADE. SOME ARE STRETCHY, OTHERS NOT; SOME ARE VERY RIGID, OTHERS VERY SOFT AND FLUID; SOME ARE TRANSPARENT, OTHERS OPAQUE; AND SOME ARE WATERPROOF. THE THREE LEADING FABRIC FAMILIES ARE AS FOLLOWS:

NATURAL FIBERS

Natural fibers come directly from nature. They come in two forms: vegetable or animal. The fibers are then spun by drawing and twisting them to obtain fabrics you can use for your garments.

PLANT FIBERS

When we think of natural plant fiber, we immediately think of cotton. Know that there are a lot of different kinds of cotton: According to their manufacturing methods, they will be more or less thick, soft, or rigid. Most cotton is easy to sew and compatible with machine sewing. Cotton garments are very breathable.

Linen, hemp, bamboo, and jute are also in this category.

ANIMAL FIBERS

There are two: wool and silk.

Silk comes from the cocoon of the silkworm.

Wool comes from the fleece of sheep, as well as from other animals:

- **Wool:** Sheep
- **Angora:** Angora rabbit
- **Camel hair:** Camel
- **Mohair:** Tibetan goat
- **Cashmere:** Indian goat
- **Alpaca:** Llama
- **Vicuña:** Peruvian llama

ARTIFICIAL FIBERS

Artificial fibers come from nature (wood, cellulose), but have been chemically treated.

THERE ARE SEVERAL KINDS:

▸ **Fibranne (viscose):** Cellulose treated in staple fibers; this gives it a "canvas look."

▸ **Rayon (viscose):** Cellulose woven with continuous threads gives it a "silk look."

▸ **Acetates and triacetates:** Treated cellulose gives it a "shiny jersey look."

SYNTHETIC FIBERS

Synthetic fibers are industrially manufactured from coal and oil.

THERE ARE 3 MAIN FAMILIES:

▸ Polyamides: Nylon, Nylfrance, Obtel, Qyana, Rilsan …

▸ Polyesters: Dacron, PET, Tergal, Terital, Terylene, Trevira … They are created to look like cotton or silk.

▸ Acrylics: Courtelle, Crylor, Dralon, Leacryl, Orlon … They reproduce the texture and appearance of wool.

BLENDS OF MATERIALS

Mixing natural and synthetic fibers allows us to take advantage of the qualities of each.

For example, the cotton/polyester blend allows us to have comfort thanks to the cotton, which lets the skin breathe, and the advantage of not wrinkling thanks to the polyester.

Fabric CHARACTERISTICS

FABRICS HAVE A FRONT AND A BACK. YOU WILL WORK ON THE WRONG (BACK) SIDE OF THE FABRIC (FOR TRACING, CUTTING, APPLYING INTERFACING, HEMMING ...) SO ONLY YOUR FLAWLESS WORK SHOWS ON THE RIGHT SIDE WHEN WORN. SO, IT IS ESSENTIAL TO ASSEMBLE THE MATERIALS BY RESPECTING THE RIGHT AND WRONG SIDES.

The feel of the fabric is also determined by how the fibers are woven. A textile is formed by crossing two sets of threads: the warp thread, which stretches vertically on the loom, and the weft thread, which passes alternately above and below the warp threads.

The straight grain noted on sewing patterns indicates the direction of the fabric fibers. The straight grain is parallel to the edges of the fabric, called selvages or "warp" direction. It is essential to respect this natural direction; to keep your garment from twisting.

The selvage runs along the edge of the fabric's lengthwise grain and can often be identified on your fabric by a stripe containing different information (such as the name of the manufacturer, designer's name, and so on). The weaving process may have left holes on the selvages, forming bumps on the right side, and hollows on the wrong side.

In craft stores, the fabric is cut across the width, **called the weft**, perpendicular to the selvage. Traditionally, the width for clothing is 55˝ (140cm), sometimes 44˝ (110cm) (for wax, Japanese or Anglo-Saxon fabrics). The patterns generally specify the quantity (length) of material necessary for a width of 55˝ (140cm) and 44˝ (110cm).

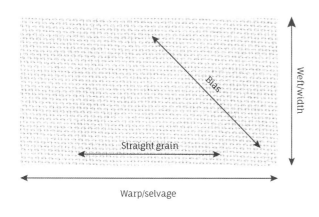

Which Fabrics FOR WHICH PROJECTS?

COTTON

There are many different kinds of cotton: According to their manufacturing methods, they will be more or less thick, soft, or rigid. Easy to sew, this textile is a thermal insulator (warm in winter and cool in summer) and breathable, like all-natural fibers.

Cotton garments are breathable, are easy-to-sew, and wear well.

FABRIC	DESCRIPTION	PARTICULARITIES	FOR WHICH PROJECTS?
BATISTE	Very fine cotton, almost transparent, soft to the touch.	Fragile.	Children's clothing, layettes, blouses, handkerchiefs, linings
BRODERIE ANGLAISE	Machine embroidery on fabric with small decorative holes at regular intervals.	x	Dresses, nightgowns, lingerie, table linens
CALICO	Rough fabric, with a regular, unbleached weave, from very fine to extremely heavy.	x	Sheets, decorative accessories, test garments for sewing.
CHAMBRAY	Cotton with a warp thread of color (gray, black, blue, or other) and a weft thread (ecru or white), which give it a slightly "mottled" side.	Easy to sew and falls nicely.	Shirts, children's clothing
CHINTZ	Thin cotton fabric with a shiny glazed side.	Falls nicely.	Dresses, curtains
STRETCH TERRY	With delicate soft loops and elastic properties (with elastane).	x	Baby clothes
COATED COTTON	Basic cotton with a waterproof coating (PUL)	x	Decorative objects, bags
CRINKLE COTTON	Delicate fabric with irregular waves.	Soft and absorbent, pleasant to wear.	Dresses, blouses
BRUSHED COTTON	Warm, fluffy fabric on one side.	x	Shirts, warm linings, children's clothing
BROADCLOTH	Fine cotton fabric, light without being transparent, the "basic" cotton fabric.	A little stretch, easy to sew, and very easy to care for.	Used for clothing (shirts, tunics)

COTTON (CONTINUED)

FABRIC	DESCRIPTION	PARTICULARITIES	FOR WHICH PROJECTS?
TICKING	Very resistant twill fabric	X	Uniforms, everyday clothes, overalls
DENIM	Denim is the classic fabric for jeans. A little thick and relatively rigid, it is most often blue or a little chambray with a blue warp thread and an ecru or white weft thread.	X	Jeans! It can also be used for home decor.
TERRY CLOTH	More rigid, less soft. It is the material of bath towels and bathrobes ... To help you differentiate it from the baby terry cloth, know that the loops are longer than the baby terry cloth.	X	Towels, bathrobes
CHEESECLOTH	Soft and loose fabric, regular weave, and a rough and brittle finish.	X	Blouses, shirts, skirts, nightwear
FLANNEL	Fluffy cotton, soft to the touch. It is not stretchy.	Soft to the touch. Frays a lot.	Children's nightwear or separates.
COTTON JERSEY	It falls nicely and does not wrinkle.	Not easy to work with. It can be sewn with a zigzag stitch; stretch stitch; or, even better, with a serger.	T-shirts, skirts or stretch dresses, tights. It is also used as a lining for winter clothing for comfort.
MADRAS	Large check fabric in bright, warm colors. It is a very cheerful fabric, fluid and delicate.	Creases easily	Clothing
MOLESKIN	One side of this firm cotton fabric has a short pile. It has a fluffy appearance.	X	Work shirts, overalls, children's pants
MUSLIN	It is used as a tailor's fabric, often to test patterns.	Simple and loose weave	Tailor's fabric used for curtains and high fashion
COTTON PIQUÉ	Cotton twill fabric with very fine grooves in the weave.	X	Suitable for bed linens or home furnishings
POPLIN	It is a very tightly woven cotton of good quality, which can sometimes give the impression of a particular shine, like satin.	It is easy to sew, supports iron-on transfers well due to its tight mesh, and is easy to care for ... Absorbent, soft, and slightly silky.	Shirts, blouses, dresses
SEERSUCKER	Light fabric with embossed stripes alternating with flat stripes.	X	Shirts, suits, children's clothing

COTTON (CONTINUED)

FABRIC	DESCRIPTION	PARTICULARITIES	FOR WHICH PROJECTS?
COTTON TWILL	The unique weave between the warp and weft threads gives it a thicker, more robust appearance.	X	Jackets, sturdy pants, work clothes, coats
CORDUROY OR FINE-RIBBED CORDUROY	A cotton fabric with a velvety appearance, but with fine grooves. Most of the time, it is 100% cotton. Relatively rigid but fluid. There are also coarse velvet ribs with wider grooves.	Easy to sew	Winter clothing such as pants, jackets, skirts, or dresses
COTTON VELVET	Regular down on the right side. Smooth hairs in one direction.	X	Evening dresses, home furnishings
COTTON VOILE	Very fine and light cotton, translucent (therefore almost transparent).	X	Children's clothing, blouses, dresses, linings (for dresses or skirts), curtains

COTTON

Cleaning: Between 100°F (40°C) and 190°F (90°C) depending on the fabric. For delicate cotton (embroidery, lace, cheesecloth …), you may need to dry-clean or hand wash them to preserve them. If you wash at 100°F (40°C) before using, they will shrink if necessary, fade, and then shrink no further.

Ironing: Steam iron on the "cotton" setting (hot to very hot). Use the "wool" setting for cotton jerseys to avoid shrinking the fabric.

FABRIC	DESCRIPTION	PARTICULARITIES	FOR WHICH PROJECTS?
LINEN	This woven fabric is made from the stems of the flax plant. It is available in different thickness levels.	This textile is a thermal insulator (warm in winter and cool in summer) and breathable, like all-natural fibers. It is more robust than cotton. It shrinks in the wash, frays a lot, and wrinkles easily.	Pants, skirts, jackets, tunics … or household linens.
LINEN BATISTE	Delicate, transparent, light, and regularly woven. Nice fall.	Pleats are more suitable than gathers.	Handkerchiefs, lingerie, blouses
THICK LINEN	Linen is made of a heavier yarn.	X	Men's suits, women's suits, pants, coats
LINEN CANVAS	Medium-weight linen with a simple weave, brittle appearance.	Strong and absorbent, pleasant to wear. Creases easily.	Shirts, skirts, dresses, pants, jackets
BAMBOO	Made from the plant's pulp, the fibers can be woven to give either an almost velvet-textured surface or spongy, springy face.	Easy to sew and maintain. In manufacture the bamboo fibers are chemically treated.	Manufacture of inserts (absorbent parts) for cloth diapers for example.
HEMP	Fibers from the plant give fabrics that can resemble some linens but are more rigid. There are hemp sponges or even fleeces.	Very strong and resistant. Easy to sew.	Sturdy clothing, home dec, home furnishings

LINEN

 Cleaning: 104°F (40°C) on a gentle cycle, dry cleaning, or by hand.

 Ironing: Steam iron on the "cotton" setting.

NATURAL ANIMAL FIBERS

FABRIC	DESCRIPTION	PARTICULARITIES	FOR WHICH PROJECTS?
SILK	Obtained from silkworms, silk is soft, delicate, and fluid, with a unique satiny hand. This light fiber needs special care.	Fragile, can stain with water. This textile is a thermal insulator (warm in winter and cool in summer) and is breathable, like all-natural fibers. It is thin and therefore not always easy to sew; it wrinkles easily.	Avoid high-wear projects.
SHANTUNG	Silk of medium thickness, simple weave, and even appearance.	X	Shirts, dresses, pants
CREPE DE CHINE	Textured, medium-thick surface	Nice fall. Cut on the bias; it gives lovely curves for evening dresses.	Evening dresses, blouses, lingerie
GEORGETTE CREPE	Loose and light fabric made of very tightly-wound fibers.	Not to be confused with its polyester "cousin."	Blouses, dresses, evening gowns
SILK DUPIONI	Fabric made of two strands of silk	Soft, fine silk with a straight or twill weave. Uneven appearance with fraying edges.	Dresses, skirts, jackets, evening wear, sheets
SILK MUSLIN	Very light, it is composed of threads with a firm twist.	Nice fall, very resilient, gathers and pleats easily. It is challenging to work with.	Evening dresses, blouses, lingerie
SILK ORGANZA	Fine transparent fabric, stiff, regular weave	Creases easily	Trimmings, collars, facings. Wedding dresses.
SILK PONGEE	Silk originating from Japan	Soft fabric available in various thicknesses	Dresses, blouses, jackets, linings
SILK SATIN / DUCHESS SATIN	Soft and satin hand. Comes in different thicknesses.	They are often striped.	Dresses, jackets, evening wear
WASHED SILK	This silk is washed in emulsifying products to remove its shine and crispness.	Nice fall	Shirts, dresses
WILD SILK	Made with the waste eliminated during the spinning process, it has an irregularity resulting from being woven with fragments of other fibers.	Easy to work with. Frays easily.	Dresses, blouses, jackets, home-furnishing accessories
TAFFETA	It has a regular grain and is soft and brittle, with very fine ribs and a glossy appearance.	Creases and wears quickly	Dresses, jackets, evening wear, wedding dresses

FABRIC	DESCRIPTION	PARTICULARITIES	FOR WHICH PROJECTS?
DEVORÉ VELVET	Treated with an acid that partially destroys its pile to create a pattern in relief	Luxurious fabric	Evening wear
WOOL	Boiled, felted, knitted, and woven, it comes from sheep's wool. This textile is a thermal insulator (warm in winter and cool in summer) and breathable. It absorbs moisture better than any other natural fiber and is fire resistant. This raw material is somewhat stretchy due to its method of manufacture (most often knitted).	It may be damaged by prolonged exposure to the sun or by mites. Challenging to care for. Wash in cold water or by hand.	Jackets, pants, skirts, coats, dresses
ALPACA	Soft, smooth, silky, loosely woven fabric	It is often mixed with other fibers that give a shine.	Coats, suits
CASHMERE	Made from the wool of the cashmere goat, it is a very soft and warm fiber—the most luxurious of all handwoven yarns.	This textile has the property of being a thermal insulator (warm) and is breathable.	Scarves, jackets, coats, men's clothing. Knitted cashmere yarn for sweaters.
CREPE	Delicate and soft, made of braided yarns, loose. Woven wool with a wavy appearance that is resistant to the touch.	X	Dresses, suits, day wear
FLANNEL	Single or cross weave, slightly velvety surface	Soft to the touch on both sides	Suits, jackets, skirts, pants
GABARDINE	Various fibers and wool qualities are used in the composition of this tightly woven fabric.	It can be challenging to work with, as it is soft and frays.	Coats, jackets, skirts, pants

SILKS

Cleaning: Dry cleaning advised!

Ironing: Dry iron on the "wool" setting. For silk satin/duchess satin, dupioni, and wild silk, steam iron on the "wool" setting with a damp cloth. Use the "wool" setting with steam but without a damp cloth for silk pongee and organza.

NATURAL ANIMAL FIBERS (CONTINUED)

FABRIC	DESCRIPTION	PARTICULARITIES	FOR WHICH PROJECTS?
SINGLE JERSEY	Single-knit fabric with horizontal ribbing on the wrong side and vertical ribbing on the right side	X	Sportswear, children's clothing, everyday wear
DOUBLE JERSEY	It has vertical ribs on both sides and is firmer than a single jersey.	It keeps you warm. Too thick for pleating.	Women's suits
WORSTED WOOL	High-quality fabric obtained by a very tight weave	Sturdy and holds its shape.	Suits, coats, home furnishings
MOHAIR	Simple weave with a hairy appearance, made from the hair of Angora goats, often mixed with wool	X	Jackets, coats, men's clothing, home furnishings. Wool for knitting sweaters.
WOOL MUSLIN	Simple weave with an uneven texture made of combed wool yarns. Light and soft fabric, often with floral patterns.	Easy to work with, nice fall	Dresses, jackets, clothing with pleats, evening wear
TARTAN	Scottish fabric with a twill weave of worsted wool, attached to a specific Scottish clan.	X	Dresses, coats, skirts, kilts, home-furnishing accessories
CLASSIC TWEED	Rough woven fabric with many colors that give it a mottled appearance	X	Suits, jackets, skirts, pants, home-furnishing accessories
MODERN TWEED	This thick fabric, a blend of large irregular wool threads, is available in a wider range of colors and patterns than traditional tweed.	X	Jackets, coats, skirts, pants, home-furnishing accessories
LEATHER AND SUEDE	Animal hide, sheep, or cowhide, tanned and treated	X	Outwear, skirts, pants, jackets, luggage

WOOL

Caution: Woolen fabrics are easy to care for but are sensitive to the sun, mites, and bleach.

Ironing: Remember to use a steam iron on the "wool" setting with a damp cloth on the back of your fabric/garment. Do not drag the iron to avoid distorting the fabric. For crepe or mohair, there is no need to use a damp cloth.

NATURAL BLENDED MATERIALS

FABRIC	DESCRIPTION	PARTICULARITIES	FOR WHICH PROJECTS?
COTTON AND SILK	Shine and drape of silk with the texture of cotton	Soft and light fabric	Dresses, shirts
WOOL AND SILK	The wool brings body and softness to the silk. Silk brings the shine.	x	Women's suits and jackets
LINEN AND SILK	Brittle linen softened by silk to give a tight, shiny fabric	Easy to work with	Women's suits, skirts, dresses, and pants
BLENDED FABRICS	This fabric's cotton-and-linen mix in yarn contains mixed warp and weft yarns. This mixture gives texture.	x	Summer jackets and dresses

SYNTHETIC FIBERS

Some fabrics are made with chemicals mixed with natural fibers and others with synthetic products.

FABRIC	DESCRIPTION	PARTICULARITIES	FOR WHICH PROJECTS?
ACETATE	This satiny fabric is made from cellulose, similar to viscose but with a different chemical composition. Other qualities: acetate taffeta, acetate satin, or acetate jersey.	It falls nicely, dyes well, washes well, and shapes with heat.	Linings, evening gowns, lingerie, sportswear
ACRYLIC	Lightweight woven or knitted fabric that looks like wool, chemically treated during manufacture.	A machine washable alternative to wool. However it retains static electricity and odors, is not very absorbant or as durable as wool.	Wovens for skirts and blouses, knits for sweaters
RUBBER	It comes from flexible and waterproof latex (the sap of rubber trees).	X	Raincoats, rainwear
CREPE	Chemically embossed fibers	Soft and supple, it is comfortable to wear.	Blouses, evening wear
FAUX SILK	It has diagonal ribs and looks like grosgrain. Made from acetate, polyester, or viscose.	Creases easily	Dresses
FAUX FUR	Imitation based on synthetic fibers, often acrylic, fixed on a woven base with body.	X	Coats, jackets, hats, bags
GROSGRAIN	Heavy, stiff fabric with a tight weave and pronounced diagonal ribbing	X	Formal wear, evening wear
JACQUARD	It has a reverse pattern on the wrong side that varies from fabric to fabric.	X	Suits, jackets, skirts
FLEECE	Lightweight fabric with a soft, fluffy appearance. It is usually made of acrylic fibers.	X	Outwear
LAMÉ	A soft, shiny, knitted, or woven fabric with one metallic thread	Mesh lamé falls better than woven lamé.	Evening dresses
LUREX	Synthetic fabric with a shiny side	Nice fall and good to work with	Evening wear

FABRIC	DESCRIPTION	PARTICULARITIES	FOR WHICH PROJECTS?
LYCRA	Made from stretch fibers, this lightweight fabric can be blended with other fibers to increase elasticity.	x	Regular clothes, sportswear
NYLON	Light, strong fabric made from polymer chips	Dyes well and is easy to wash. Nonabsorbent, retains static electricity, and sticks to the skin.	Rainwear, skiwear, underwear
PVC	Lightweight woven or knitted fabric coated with polyvinyl chloride, making it strong and nonporous	x	Trimmings, rainwear, aprons
FLOCKED FABRIC	Synthetic or blended fabric with irregularities that form patterns	x	Dresses, jackets, evening wear
EMBOSSED FABRIC	Transparent, stiff, and finely pleated synthetic fabric with an embossed appearance	Delicate to sew	Evening dresses
SEQUINED FABRIC	Lightweight fabric with sequins attached	Sequins are heat sensitive and tarnish quickly.	Evening dresses
TULLE	A kind of nylon mesh	Causes irritation. It cannot be worn next to the skin.	Large skirts, dance tutus, costumes
VELVET	This fabric has a velvety appearance, is easy to sew, and is generally warm. It can be made of polyester, acrylic, or a cotton/polyester blend.	x	Skirts, dresses, jackets, pants ...
VINYL	Heavy and synthetic nonwoven fabric that looks like leather	Does not breathe like leather	Sofas, armchairs, outdoor clothing
POLYESTER	This 100% synthetic material is available in many forms.	Thermal insulator (therefore hot). It can let moisture through without getting wet: it dries very quickly.	x
POLYESTER CREPE	Soft and robust fabric	It does not wrinkle; nice fall.	Lingerie, blouses, dresses, evening wear
MICROFIBER	Very tightly woven fabric composed of delicate fibers	Made to last. Some types are waterproof.	All kinds of clothing

SYNTHETIC FIBERS (CONTINUED)

FABRIC	DESCRIPTION	PARTICULARITIES	FOR WHICH PROJECTS?
MINKY	Stretchy textile very close to polar fleece but with a "plush" appearance. It is available with raised motifs (polka dots, stars, hearts ...) and in all colors.	X	Soft comforters or liners for children's blankets
NICKY VELOUR	Velvet look. Soft and stretchy, it has a somewhat satiny, even shiny, appearance.	X	Children's pajamas, cozy indoor clothing, comforters
FLEECE	It is stretchy.	It is easy to maintain and doesn't fray, so you can leave its edges "raw."	Sweaters, jackets, robes, blankets, warm linings for clothes
SUEDE	Looks and feels like tanned leather with its velvety, soft feel. Non-stretchy, washable at 86°F (30°C), a little thick, and quite stiff.	X	Skirts, dresses, jackets, pants ...
POLYESTER	Fabric made to look and feel like canvas	It holds creases and requires less maintenance than cotton.	Tablecloths, curtains, cushion covers

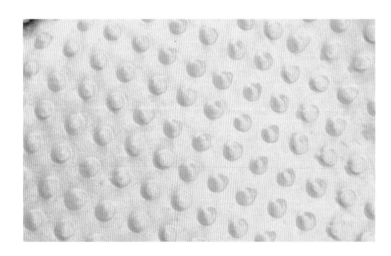

SYNTHETIC FABRICS

 Cleaning: Dry clean, hand wash, or at 100°F (40°C) depending on the fabric.

 Ironing: Steam iron on the "wool" setting; you can increase the heat after testing a small corner of the fabric. Otherwise, you risk melting the fabric.

SYNTHETIC BLEND MATERIALS

FABRIC	DESCRIPTION	PARTICULARITIES	FOR WHICH PROJECTS?
BOUCLÉ	Loosely knitted or woven, it is composed of curly and looped yarns that give a voluminous appearance. Blend of viscose, polyester, or wool.	x	Women's suits
CHARMEUSE	Delicate, with a satin appearance, this fabric is shiny on the front and matte on the back. It is made of rayon, viscose, polyester, or blended fibers.	x	Blouses, lingerie
SATIN CREPE	Satin on one side and crepe on the other. It is made of rayon, polyester, and silk.	Falls nicely.	Dresses, blouses, lingerie
JERSEY	It is manufactured using a knitted method so that a jersey can be made of cotton and viscose (basically from wood fibers but ultimately synthetic) or a cotton/polyester/elastane blend, for example.	Avoid using "acrylic!" You will perspire in it but not necessarily get hot ...	Depending on its thickness and elasticity, it is possible to make T-shirts, panties, sweatshirts, tracksuits, pants ...
VISCOSE	Also called rayon. Made from wool pulp or cotton fluff mixed with chemicals.	Easy to sew, absorbent, and shrink resistant. It falls nicely, does not retain static electricity, and dyes easily. Does not fray.	Dresses, skirts, blouses, jackets

CHOOSING
Your Fabric

FABRIC STORES ARE A TREASURE TROVE FOR SEWISTS. TAKE THE TIME TO VISIT A FEW CRAFT STORES OR WEBSITES TO GET A FEEL FOR THE DIFFERENT TYPES OF FABRIC. FABRIC OPTIONS ARE ENDLESS, BUT THERE ARE TWO BASIC TYPES: GARMENTS AND HOME FURNISHINGS. IN MANY CASES THESE FABRICS CAN BE INTERCHANGEABLE.

Whether you're buying fabric for garments or home furnishings, you will need a clear idea of what you're looking for in terms of composition, colors, and patterns. For patterns, assess compare the color combinations and evaluate the pattern repeats. Feel the fabric and test its drape. Does the fabric have body and support, or is it soft and floaty? As a final point, take a look at the care instructions. The fabric should be suitable for its intended use.

Questions to ask yourself before you buy

▸ Is the fabric suitable for my project?

▸ Do the care instructions match my intended use?

▸ Is the density and drape of the fabric right for my project?

▸ Do the patterns match my project?

▸ Does the pattern or material work with this project?

▸ What is the width of this fabric?

SHOULD I CHOOSE COTTON FABRIC TO START WITH?

When you start sewing, there are many things to discover and master: the sewing machine, thread, needles, hand sewing, fabrics, patterns (tracing and understanding), and mastering the speed and direction of the machine ...

To practice and make your first projects, definitely use cotton without spandex. It is easy to handle, cut, and sew. It will be the ideal companion for your first creations. You will be able to make tote bags, cushions, accessories, and your first simple clothes ...

SEWING DIFFICULT FABRICS

Each fabric has its own characteristics: a look, feel, and texture that require specific sewing tools. Before handling a fabric, ask yourself what you need in terms of a machine foot, needle, stitches, or thread. Here is a list of fabrics for hand or machine sewing with some advice and tips for each one:

▸ **Jersey:** Used to make T-shirts, sweatshirts, tops, or light dresses, this knitted fabric has a stretchy texture, sometimes with spandex, which adds elasticity and stretch which means a little extra care in tracing patterns or cutting pieces.

To sew jersey, use a special jersey or stretch machine needle. Choose the needle size according to the thickness of the jersey. You will also find double needles in craft stores that are specially designed for this type of fabric; they allow you to stitch stretchy hems with the appearance of two parallel rows of straight stitching.

Be careful not to sew jersey with a conventional straight stitch; otherwise, you will lose the elasticity of the fabric and pull and break the seam. If possible, use the "stretch" stitches on your machine, and do not pull on the fabric when stitching! Ideally, stick to cotton sewing thread when sewing a cotton jersey. The serger is the ideal machine for sewing jersey fabric.

▸ **Denim:** When thick, it requires a special machine needle sold in sewing and craft stores, but a simple standard needle, size 100, will also do. Some machines have special feet for thick materials; make sure to check your accessories! Topstitch your denim project to reinforce it and for clean edges. There are special, stronger threads designed for sewing denim.

▸ **Leather:** More commonly used for leather goods, it is available in thinner or imitation leather for garments such as jackets, skirts, or pants. You will find special machine needles in sewing and craft stores, but if you choose a thicker leather, hand sewing is required with a curved needle specially designed for leather. Use a thicker thread to avoid breaking the thread when sewing. It is recommended that you use a dual-feed foot. If you do not have one, place a piece of parchment paper between your fabric and the foot of your machine.

▸ **Delicate fabrics:** Lightweight fabrics that require special attention include muslin, organza, voile, batiste, and various synthetic fibers. Lightweight fabrics tend to slide off the table when cutting. Cover the table with a sheet of tissue paper or place tissue paper under the fabric, and cut the fabric and paper together. If you're working with fluid fabrics, it's best to reconstruct your entire pattern and cut it out on a single layer. To do this, place your half-pattern on your unfolded fabric with the back facing you. Trace the first half and then flip it 180° and trace the other half symmetrically.

Use fine pins to attach the pattern pieces to the fabric: Place them close together at the seam allowance so they don't mark the main parts of the work. With sharp scissors, make notches on the outside—not on the inside if the seam allowances, as usual.

Mark the pattern markings with a tailor's tack, made by hand with a fine needle and thread. Stitch with small and short, but loose, stitches. To simplify sewing, you can attach tissue paper to each piece before stitching when working with a challenging, slippery fabric. This will prevent the fabric from puckering during machine sewing.

Choose a size 70 needle or smaller and cotton thread. To prevent the fabric from puckering while sewing, do not use the backstitch but tie your threads together to secure the seams.

▸ **Coated or waxed fabric:** Thicker than regular fabric, it also tends to catch the needle when sewing. To simplify sewing, use a size 90 needle and a stronger polyester thread. Use a Teflon presser foot for machine sewing, or stick a piece of tape on the underside of your regular machine foot to prevent slippage. If you are having trouble, place adhesive tape (such as masking tape) on the fabric, stitch on it, and remove the tape after the seam is made. Don't use pins that will leave small holes in the fabric. Iron the fabric on the back side only!

▸ **Cotton gauze and double gauze** are very trendy and have an embossed look, but they fray quickly. It is imperative to overcast them.

▸ **Faux fur:** To simplify the work, trim the edges of the faux fur by ⅜″ (1cm). If attaching to fabric, pin to the faux fur, right sides together. Stitch the two layers together then turn to the right side out and use a needle to catch any stubborn hairs trapped in the seam. Stitch the fabrics together.

▸ **Velvet** has a directional pile and looks different depending on its direction (brighter or darker). When cutting velvet, ensure that all the pieces face the same direction. Otherwise, they will look like they were cut from two different fabrics. Be aware that velvet is very fluffy. Mark the fabric with chalk or a tailor's basting stitch on the back of the fabric. Baste the pieces together along the lengthy seams. To stitch, choose a needle—preferably a new one—for the thickness of the fabric and use a dual-feed, Teflon, or roller foot. These presser feet simplify the process of keeping the two pieces of fabric together during stitching. If possible, reduce the tension of the presser foot to avoid damaging the hairs: You can even use a narrower zipper presser foot. The velvet should not be pushed or pulled under the presser foot of the machine, but it should be held firmly. Place your hands flat on either side of the presser foot, as close to the presser foot as possible. Iron the velvet on the wrong side of the fabric; otherwise, the pile will be damaged and

permanent marks will be left. If ironing on the right side of the fabric is necessary, consider using a damp cloth.

▸ **PUL (Polyurethane Laminate)** is a slippery material and is not very easy to sew. Using a dual feed will simplify the sewing process. You can also use a Teflon presser foot, which reduces the slippery aspect. Alternatively, place a sheet of tracing paper between the PUL and the presser foot. When you are finished sewing, tear off the paper.

PATTERNS

ESSENTIAL FOR MAKING CLOTHING MODELS, THE SEWING PATTERN CAN SOMETIMES LOOK VERY COMPLICATED WITH ALL THE INDICATIONS AND MARKERS. THE MORE YOU WORK WITH PATTERNS, THE EASIER THEY ARE TO READ. OVER TIME THE CODES AND CONSTRUCTION TECHNIQUES WILL BECOME MORE FAMILIAR TO YOU. THE SAME IS TRUE FOR THE INSTRUCTION ILLUSTRATIONS.

A pattern is a flat representation of the pieces that make up a garment or project. It is used to cut and assemble the different pieces of fabric that come together to make the final product.

There are many patterns in envelopes (with one or two designs), in books, in magazines, and published on the internet. For the latter, it may be necessary to print all the pieces onto letter paper and put them together like a puzzle, or have a copyshop print the pattern on large-format paper. Some patterns can also be drawn out on a squared grid. It is necessary to expand this reduced pattern to the actual size by enlarging the measurements. For example, a ⅜″ (1cm) tile on a grid sheet may represent 2″ (5cm) in an actual size.

Pattern making has different levels so that you can choose according to your personal taste and skills. It is better to start with easy patterns and progress than to tackle patterns that are too complicated and get discouraged.

PATTERN PIECES

Patterns are usually drawn on large sheets of paper that include all garment and project pieces.

Today, most patterns include several sizes. Different lines identify each size. Locate the lines that correspond to your measurements if this information is given, and refer to the legends to see which pattern line matches your size.

Each piece is identified with the name of the pattern (skirt, pants, and so on), the name of the pattern (front, back), necessary markings (straight grain, clip), and the cutting instructions (cut × 1, fold, clip, and so on).

THE SYMBOLS

Each pattern piece contains several symbols that will help you assemble your work. These symbols are found in all pattern brands.

HOW TO DO IT

The patterns come with essential instructions, including:

▸ The type of fabric to buy
▸ The amount of fabric needed per size
▸ The length of a possible lining
▸ Supplies (elastic, buttons, and etc.)
▸ The width of the seam allowance

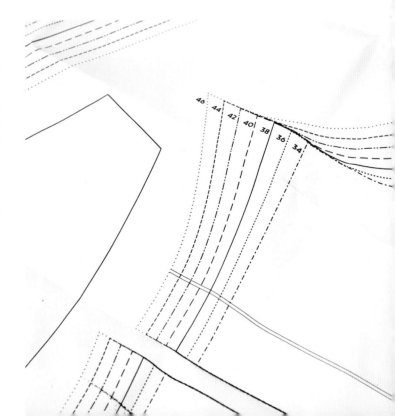

ABOUT

THE SEWING MACHINE

TO GET THE MOST OUT OF YOUR SEWING MACHINE, IT'S BEST TO KNOW
EVERYTHING ABOUT IT. TAKE TIME TO STUDY HOW IT WORKS: READ
THE INSTRUCTIONS, PRACTICE SEWING, AND USE THE ACCESSORIES.
YOU'LL SOON DISCOVER THAT YOU CAN DO ALL SORTS OF THINGS
THAT TAKE LONGER TO DO BY HAND.

How to Choose
YOUR FIRST
SEWING MACHINE

RECOMMENDED STITCHES AND FUNCTIONS

The most important thing is to determine what features you will need.

▸ There's no point in buying something too sophisticated if you're not sure you'll enjoy sewing, but your machine still needs to be robust.

▸ Ideally, it should be easy to use and offer enough possibilities to allow you to progress further.

▸ You must consider what you want to sew before buying a sewing machine!

THE ESSENTIAL STITCHES
WHEN STARTING OUT

▸ **The straight stitch** (length adjustment required, depending on the fabric) is the stitch sewists use all the time.

▸ **The zigzag stitch** (length/width adjustment), which often has a default of 2 or 3 sizes, prevents the fabric from fraying. You can also use it to sew elastic fabrics (jersey or knitwear).

▸ **The three-step zigzag stitch** allows you to sew elastics easily.

▸ **The semi-automatic four-step or one-step buttonhole** makes things easier and is very useful when sewing clothes or home dec items like cushions.

OTHER VERY USEFUL FUNCTIONS

▸ **Tension adjustment** allows you to adjust the tension of the thread on the top of the machine for the needle thread and on the bobbin for the bottom thread.

▸ **The stitch length adjustment** allows you to adapt your sewing to the thickness of the fabric, to sew gathers, or to baste ...

THE LITTLE EXTRAS THAT CAN BE CONSIDERED AS GADGETS:

▸ **The automatic needle threader** (Note: There are also manual threaders.)

▸ **The bobbin in a horizontal position.** It's easier to install than the vertical bobbin.

NOTE

Don't buy a machine just because it offers dozens and dozens of stitches ... Often this is just a simple "variation" of the width and length of the same stitch in four or five varieties (the straight stitch with the needle on the left, middle or right; a zigzag stitch of different lengths or widths).

TIP

Finding a machine with at least these essential stitches will allow you to sew properly and make clean finishes while having fun.

COMPUTERIZED OR MECHANICAL?

Now that you have an idea of what you want to sew, the machine choice will be based on your budget. The budget is even more important if you don't know exactly what you want to make.

If you want to spend about $100, you can choose a mechanical machine. For your first steps, this can be more than enough.

But if you are sure of yourself and can afford electronic machines immediately, take advantage of it! On the other hand, you will have trouble finding a computerized machine below $200.

THE ADVANTAGES OF COMPUTERIZED MACHINES

▶ More intuitive sewing: Minimal adjustment is required but can be modified.

▶ Stitches are finished automatically.

▶ The needle can be stopped when it is raised or lowered.

▶ Automatic buttonholes: You don't have to touch anything.

▶ Speed limiter (very safe) on a large number of models.

▶ Silent sewing machines: Test depending on the brand.

THE DISADVANTAGES

▶ They can seem complicated for beginners because of the screen and the various keys.

▶ They may be not quite as sturdy as mechanical machines and not as suitable for travel.

If you don't have anyone around you to give you advice, it is often better to go to a specialized store to get all the information you need to make your choice. Take the opportunity to test the machines in the store.

Buying on online can be economically attractive. These websites also offer free shipping and additional accessories or interesting discounts. You can also read up on internet forums and blogs to compare brands you are interested in.

Beware of buying in big box stores; they do not always provide optimal after-sales service.

At most machine retailers, you can find used sewing machines that have been serviced and are under warranty: Don't hesitate! A good used machine is better than a poor-quality new one!

▶ **Captions:**

1: Thread guides
2: Stitch length dial
3: Bobbin winder
4: Handwheel
5: Stitch selector
6: Needle
7: Needle plate

How a SEWING MACHINE WORKS

THE THREAD

The machine needs 2 threads to be able to sew:

- **The thread that comes off the spool, located on the top of the machine**
- **The bobbin thread, located near the bottom of the machine**

These 2 threads will intertwine to form a stitch.

Check the tension of the thread on a sample of fabric identical to the fabric you will use for your project. This will help you have a nice stitch above and below your work.

WHEN AND HOW TO ADJUST THE THREAD TENSION

The tension is usually set between 4 and 6, depending on the machine. When you first sew, check your stitches: If they look good on the top and bottom, the tension is correct. The thread should slide easily off the spool, and the metal discs should not be too tight. It is rare to have to change this setting.

It will be necessary to change the tension if the stitches are not pretty and even, or when you need to change the thickness of the thread (such as extra-strong thread for topstitching jeans or a very thin thread such as silk thread).

You will need to lower the thread tension if you are sewing mesh or jersey:

- If sewing relaxes the fabric and creates a bulge.
- If you are sewing hems with a twin needle and this also creates bulging.

THREADING THE MAIN THREAD

Sewing machines, whether mechanical or computerized, can be differentiated by how the spool pin is attached (horizontally or vertically) and how the bobbin is placed (horizontally or vertically).

Within each brand, there are different sewing machines. Selecting machines from the same brand does not guarantee the same direction of the spindle or the same way of positioning the bobbin.

1. Place the spool on its axis above the sewing machine.

- You don't need to do anything else when the axis is vertical.
- If the spindle is horizontal, place a spool cover with a diameter close to the spool to hold it.

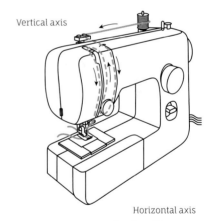

Vertical axis

Horizontal axis

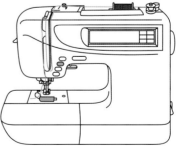

2. Feed the thread from the spool through the guide(s) on the top of the machine. On newer machines, all guides are numbered for your convenience.

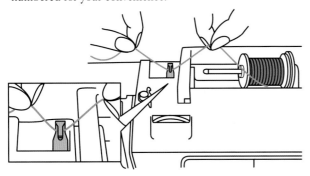

3. Continue feeding the thread down the machine and through a metal loop. If you need a little slack in your thread, feel free to turn the handwheel on the right side of the machine towards you.

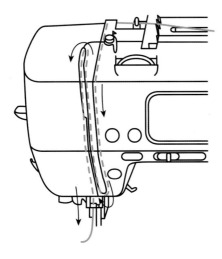

4. Once through the loop, bring the thread down and through a final hook near the needle.

5. Pass the thread through the eye of the needle from the front to the back of the machine.

6. Pass the thread under the presser foot and pull it toward the back of your machine.

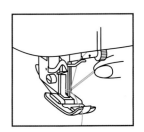

THREADING THE BOBBIN THREAD

When you want to sew, it is essential to install your bobbin correctly. Installing a bobbin incorrectly is one of the first mistakes you'll make when starting out. One of the basic rules of machine sewing is to sew with the same thread on the bobbin and the spool. Otherwise, you will never get the thread tension right.

THERE ARE TWO MAIN TYPES OF BOBBINS:

▸ Horizontal-loading bobbins
▸ Vertical-loading bobbins

Horizontal-loading bobbins are the easiest to install.

When installing a bobbin in your machine, it is essential to respect the direction of the thread. The bobbin thread should be wound counterclockwise.

1. For horizontal-loading bobbins, position the bobbin in the bobbin case and follow the markings on your machine to bring the thread out.

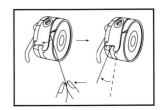

Replace the plastic cover.

2. For vertical-loading bobbins, position the bobbin in the bobbin case and feed the thread through the slot in the bobbin case.

The Different
EQUIPMENT

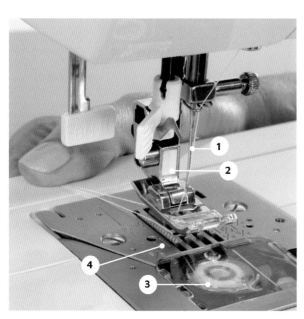

1 - Needle 2 - Presser foot 3 - Bobbin 4 - Needle plate

FOR BOTH TYPES OF BOBBINS:

▸ Lock the bobbin by opening the tab on the back of the bobbin case and inserting it into the machine.

▸ To pull the bobbin thread out of the opening under the presser foot, hold the bobbin thread in your left hand.

▸ With your right hand, turn the handwheel on the right side of your machine towards you to lower the needle.

▸ When the two threads form a loop, pick them up with a ruler or a pair of scissors.

Pull the threads free to the back of the machine.

THE BOBBINS

When shopping, invest in bobbins. The more bobbins you have, the more time you save, especially since it is a minimal investment.

THE NEEDLES

Each sewing project must be made with a suitable fabric and the right needle (type and size).

▸ **The diameter of the needle is expressed in 100th of a millimeter:** A US size 14 (size 90) needle is 90/100 of a millimeter.

▸ **The universal needle** for domestic machines is usually 130/705 H (fine ballpoint).

▸ Needles are numbered from 60/8 to 110/18 and are sold in sets or by size. The size of a needle is engraved on its shank and its box.

THE MOST COMMON TYPES OF NEEDLES

STANDARD (OR UNIVERSAL) NEEDLES

▸ They are used for most natural and synthetic fabrics. The point is slightly rounded to sew all materials.
▸ When you buy a sewing machine, several needles are supplied with it, usually in size 80/12 or 90/14.
▸ Needle sizes range from 60/8 to 100/16.

SPECIAL NEEDLES

▸ **Microtex:** The point is sharp and fine to simplify the perforation of very fine fabrics or very dense materials such as microfiber fabric, silk, sequin fabric, nylon, polyester, poplin, organza, and taffeta. Needle sizes range from 60/8 to 80/12.

▸ **Denim:** The point is extremely fine to penetrate thick and tight fabrics more easily without damaging the material. The shaft is reinforced to avoid deflecting, breaking, or skipping stitches. Needle sizes range from 90/14 to 110/18.

▶ **Leather:** The tip is sharp to pierce leather more easily. Use on leather, faux leather, and suede. Needle sizes range from 80/12 to 100/16.

▶ **Jersey:** The point is rounded to slide through the fabric without breaking the fibers. It is essential for jerseys and Lycra, and keeps the seam elastic. Needle sizes range from 70/10 (for Lycra and fine jersey) to 90/14.

▶ **Stretch:** The tip is ball shaped (stretch) to slide through the fabric without breaking the fibers. It also prevents hems from curling too much. It is essential for all knitted fabrics. Needle sizes range from 75/11 to 90/14.

DOUBLE NEEDLES (OR TWIN NEEDLES)

Double needles are used to make hems with double stitching and can be used on most sewing machines. They are ideal for sewing stretch materials such as jersey because they keep the elasticity of the stitch while maintaining the look of two rows of straight stitching. There are several types depending on the fabric to be sewn. Needle sizes range from 75/11 to 90/14.

TO REMEMBER

The higher the number, the more the needle adapts to thick fabrics. To sew a dense fabric like denim, it is better to choose a thick needle (100/16, for example) that will not break or a special denim needle.

The lighter the fabric, the finer the weave and the fibers. For light fabric, you should use thin needles to avoid breaking the fibers and creating holes.

WHAT SIZE NEEDLE SHOULD I CHOOSE?

▶ Size 60/8 is suitable for silk.

▶ Size 70/10 is perfect for fine cotton or materials that "fear holes," such as coated waterproof fabrics.

▶ Sizes 80/12 to 90/14 are suitable for most clothing fabrics.

▶ Size 100/16 is often used for denim.

▶ Increase the number for thicker fabrics, home furnishings, or when you need to sew more than two layers.

CHANGE YOUR NEEDLES REGULARLY.

The life of a sewing machine needle is shorter than you might think. A needle generally has a life of 8 hours (or less if you sew thick fabrics). The easiest way to estimate your needle's quality is to gently touch the tip with your finger. If you feel tiny bumps, the needle needs to be changed.

If you can't tell the difference between a new and a damaged needle (it will come with practice), consider changing it every 3 to 4 projects, depending on their size.

WHY DOES YOUR NEEDLE BREAK?

▶ The needle is twisted and caught by the hook.

▶ The needle is twisted by the bobbin, which is poorly positioned, and drags it.

▶ The needle has been chosen incorrectly and is too thin for the thickness of the sewn fabric.

▶ The needle is too thin for the thickness of the thread.

▶ This can also happen if you put too much force on your fabric.

▶ The needle quickly passes over the pins placed vertically on the fabric, but sometimes, with speed, it can hit one of them and break.

OVERVIEW TABLE

MATERIALS	TYPES DE MATIÈRES	THICKNESS	NEEDLE TYPE	NEEDLE DIAMETER	THREAD TYPE	LABEL NUMBER (THREAD WEIGHT)
WOVEN	Fine fabrics, organza, tulle, voile	Fine	130/705H	60/8–70/10	Polyester or cotton	120–100
	Silks, cotton, voile, poplin, crepe, taffeta, lace, underwear	Semi-fine	130/705H	70/10	Polyester or cotton	100
	Crepe, poplin, satins, cottons and woolens, gingham, taffeta, velvet, blouses, dresses, linings	Medium	130/705H	80/12	Polyester or cotton	100–60
	Woolen clothing, dresses, skirts, coats, tweeds, sheets, linens, jeans	Medium-heavy	130/705H-J	80/12–90/14	Polyester or cotton	80–40
	Coarse cloth, thick woolens, blankets, coats, jeans, clothing, home-furnishing fabrics, work wear	Heavy	130/705H-J		Polyester or cotton	40
LEATHER AND IMITATION LEATHER, ELASTIC	Soft leathers	Medium	130/705H-LR	90/14–100/16	Polyester or cotton	60
	Suede, calfskin, goatskin	Medium	130/705H-LR	90/14–100/16		60
	Imitation leather, plastic materials	Medium	130/705H-LL	90/14–100/16		60–40
	Vinyl type	Medium-heavy	130/705H-LL	80/12–100/16		60–40
	Waxed cloth	Medium-heavy	130/705H-LL	80/12–100/16		60–40
KNITWEAR, STRETCH	Knitwear, jersey, underwear	Fines	130/705H-S	80/12–90/14	Polyester or cotton	80
	Stretch velvet, jersey, interlock, medium knits	Medium	130/705H-S	60/8–100/16		80–90
	Jersey and stretch clothing, significant knits, elastic materials, hosiery	Medium-heavy	130/705H-SUK	60/8–80/12		90–100

THE PEDAL

The pedal is the gas pedal of your machine; it is the link to the device's engine. Imagine a car.

▶ To move forward, press the pedal. The smoother you are, the better the seam will look and the easier it will be to steer your fabric.

▶ If you want to go backward, press the button/rod to make the feed dogs go in the opposite direction.

▶ To stop, lift your foot.

THE FEED DOGS

When you are new to sewing, steering the fabric is one of your challenges. We always want to do something with our hands, pulling or pushing our fabric, but the feed dogs on the machine are there to do that job. The more you want to "help the fabric feed" the more you'll interfere with the action of the feed dogs.

▶ The more feed dogs you have, the easier and more evenly the fabric will slide under the foot of your machine.

▶ 3 to 7 feed dogs are ideal.

THE MAIN FEET

▶ **The basic presser foot, or straight-stitch presser foot,** creates the majority of stitches and will be the foot you use most often. You can do straight stitches, zigzag stitches, or decorative stitches.

▶ **The zipper foot** is essential for sewing any zipper. It will also be useful for piping cushions or bags.

▶ **The buttonhole foot** is used to make beautiful buttonholes for all sizes of buttons.

TO REMEMBER

The width of a classic presser foot is ³⁄₁₆″ (0.5cm)—useful for sewing all the seams that must be made ³⁄₁₆″ (0.5cm) from the edge!

THE SPECIFIC OPTIONS

▶ **Invisible zipper foot:** This is a unique foot for attaching invisible zippers. Without it, it is challenging to get an excellent finish.

▶ **The dual-feed, also called even-feed, foot:** This is very useful for thick fabrics or certain elastic fabrics.

This foot feeds the fabric both top and bottom. It's a little expensive, so only buy it if you sew a lot of thick fabrics. There are many more: bias foot, hem foot, overlock foot, fringe foot, gathering foot ...

The COMPLETE MANUAL OF Sewing

PART II

TECHNIQUES

FROM THE FIRST STITCH TO THE LAST BUTTON

First STEPS IN SEWING:
GETTING READY TO SEW

DETERMINING YOUR SIZE

First, forget about the size you're used to buying in ready-to-wear clothing.

Brands—whether pattern brands or off-the-shelf clothing brands—use their own templates (sometimes called slopers or base patterns), as a starting point for all designs. For women, the four basic patterns are for the bodice, the skirt, the pants, and the sleeve. Each brand uses its own base patterns based on its own set of standard measurements. A size M in one brand will not necessarily correspond to a size M in another brand!

Therefore, you must choose the garment size according to your measurements. Each pattern includes a measurement table, listing the corresponding measurements in inches and/or centimeters for each size.

TIP

For tops and dresses, the main measurement is the chest size.

For skirts and pants, the waist and hip measurements are most important.

Ideally, have someone else take your measurements.

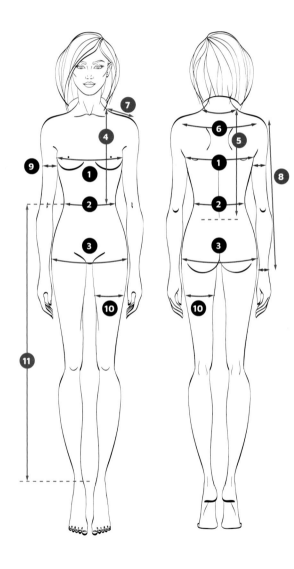

PROCEDURES TO FOLLOW

▸ When you measure yourself, do it without clothes (you can quickly add an inch or a few centimeters to account for your jeans or sweater, but wear a bra if you normally do) with a flexible tape measure. Before starting, place a tape around your waist; this will be the basis for measuring your verticals. Ensure the tape measure is horizontal and does not fall or curl in the back.

▸ **1. Chest circumference.** Position the tape measure horizontally at the widest part of the chest.

▸ **2. Waist circumference.** The tape measure should be positioned at the narrowest point.

▸ **3. Hip circumference.** The measurement should be taken at the widest part of the hips and buttocks.

▸ **4. Bust height.** From the base of your neck to your bustline (where you measured chest circumference).

▸ **5. Back height.** From the base of the neck to your waistband on the back.

▸ **6. Back width.** From one arm to the other across and over the shoulder blades. With your arms down, measure from one underarm to the other at the point of the shoulder blades.

▸ **7. Shoulder length.** Measure from the base of the neck to the top of the shoulder.

▸ **8. Arm length.** From the top of the shoulder to the wrist, arm extended.

▸ **9. The arm circumference.** Taken at the widest part.

▸ **10. The thigh circumference.** It is also taken at the widest part of the thigh.

▸ **11. Leg length.** From your waistband to the ankle.

Then choose the size you need to sew in the pattern's measurement table. If you are between two sizes in the measurement table, take the larger one. It is always possible to remove excess fabric but trying to add fabric once it has been cut away is impossible.

Before you start doing anything with the fabric, it is essential to prepare it.

The first step is to wash and iron it, for several reasons:

▶ The fabrics you find are likely to have traveled and been stored in warehouses before arriving at your home. Washing them will help get rid of dust.

▶ Some production finishes, such as those used in the finishing of the fabric, are also removed during the cleaning process.

▶ This stabilizes the fabric (size and color in particular). Some fabrics can move a lot during this first wash (linen, knitwear), and skipping this preliminary step can lead to significant disappointment (shrinkage of your work in the first wash, damage).

▶ Wash your fabric using the setting you will use for your finished garment.

Ironing helps you put the fibers back in place and avoid having a wrinkled fabric that will distort your cut. Set the iron temperature and test on a sample of the fabric. Be careful not to stretch your fabric too much during this operation: The fibers may be irreparably stretched and not come back into place. Also, be sure to adjust the iron's temperature for fragile fabrics. Always iron on the back side and use a damp cloth—a piece of cotton cloth or tea towel placed between the material and the iron.

The second step is to check that the fabric is on the straight grain. To do this, lay the fabric out on a flat surface and check to see if the edges of the fabric are perfectly straight. If they are not, trim the edges by trimming the fabric 4″ (10cm) and, using a pin, release and pull a weft thread across the width of the fabric. Cut using this thread as a guide to cut across the rest of the fabric piece.

▶ **If the weave has been twisted in the weft,** fold the fabric on the bias if the distortion is slight. Hold the ends and pull the fabric in short strokes. Lay the fabric flat to ensure that the selvages are perfectly aligned. If there is significant distortion, fold the fabric in half lengthwise, with the back side facing out. Pin to the selvage. Using an iron or the flat of your hand, flatten the fabric's surface, straightening the fabric so that the edges are parallel.

TIP

To avoid disappointment, get into the habit of putting your new fabric directly into the laundry basket as soon as you get home from the store. Ideally, it is best to do this as soon as you buy it, so it will be folded and stored and ready to use. Iron it and keep it stored with the back of the fabric visible to prevent it from fading in the light.

COPYING A PATTERN

Trace the pattern in your size to keep the original version unaltered and to make a working version so you can make changes, annotations, and so on.

▶ **You must copy EVERYTHING as if you were making a manual photocopy of your pattern:** text, lines, part number, marks, and notches.

The latter is very important for the rest of your project. Notches are used to connect two pieces of clothing during assembly or to position a piece correctly (notches to distinguish the front and back of a sleeve, for example). If you don't respect the notches during assembly because you haven't copied them correctly, it can distort the construction of your work.

▸ We suggest you to attach tacing paper over the pattern with masking tape so that it does not shift during the tracing. You must be as precise as possible to avoid adding or removing fractions of an inch or a few millimeters.

▸ **For straight lines, use a ruler. For curves, make points at regular intervals rather than drawing them entirely:** This will make cutting out your pattern on fabric more accurate.

▸ Be aware that if the seam allowances are not included, they must be added at this stage, everywhere except on the fold lines. If you are splitting any pattern pieces—to fit into a fabric swatch or to make yokes, for example—remember to add the seam allowances.

To do this, draw a line parallel to the pattern line using an acrylic ruler, for example. Take evenly spaced points on the initial line and mark a perpendicular mark at the distance of the seam allowance (⅝″/1.5cm, for example). Join these marks so that the line is parallel to the initial line. Remember to mark each piece of your pattern with the added seam allowance.

▸ Once all the pieces have been traced on paper, cut them out with paper scissors.

SOME MODIFICATIONS

You can correct specific points when the pattern does not match your measurements. Some changes are straightforward and can be made from your first sewing project; others require more skill and are not covered here.

LENGTHEN OR SHORTEN A PATTERN PIECE

A pattern should typically include a line (or two closely spaced lines) perpendicular to the straight grain that allows you to shorten or lengthen the pattern pieces.

The method is the same whether you are working on a bust, pants, or sleeve piece.

1. To lengthen a piece, cut along this line, spread the two pieces of the pattern apart, and insert a strip of paper the height of the number of inches/centimeters you wish to add. You can use graph paper to cut out this strip to ensure accurate measurements. Tape it between the two pattern pieces and trim the sides.

2. To shorten a piece, draw a line parallel to the line on the pattern, with the distance between the two lines being the distance you want to take off the pattern. Fold the line on the pattern up to the line you drew. Tape and trim the sides.

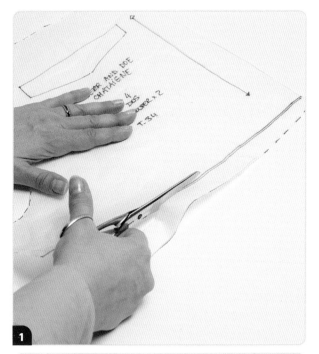

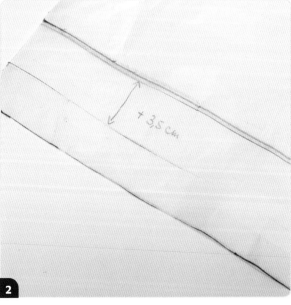

MINI PATTERN GLOSSARY

Back side/front side: To help position your fabric on the fabric's right side (top) or wrong side (bottom).

Straight grain: Position the pieces in the direction of the straight grain—that is, parallel to the edge of the fabric—to keep the material's structure intact.

Fabric on the fold: These indicate where the fabric should be folded with the pattern placed on the fold line (which should not be cut) to obtain a symmetrical piece.

MIXING SIZES

In real life, our bodies are far from standardized; your measurements may be a mix of several sizes. Thus, you can make a 38 in the chest and waist and a 40 in the hips, for example.

Sewing allows you to mix sizes easily and adjust a pattern to your actual measurements.

1. On your pattern, add a small mark on the bust, waist, or hip lines on the line corresponding to the size determined by the measurement (for example, 38 at the bust and 40 at the hips).

2. Join these different points with a colored line by bending the curves (using a curved ruler).

3. Copy the pattern by tracing this new line.

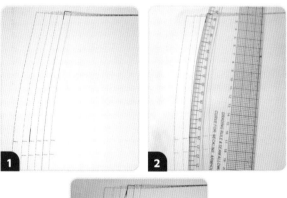

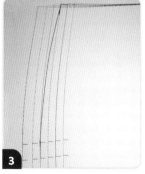

MOVING A CHEST DART

The height of the bust line varies according to body type. It may be necessary to raise or lower the chest dart.

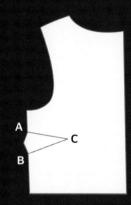

To do this, consider the triangle of the dart as a whole (A, B, and C).

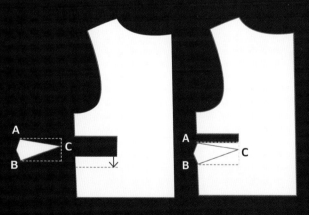

Determine how much you want the dart moved then cut it out. Note that if you move the point ¾″ (2cm) down (or up), you will have to move the other two points of the triangle ¾″ (2cm) down (or up).

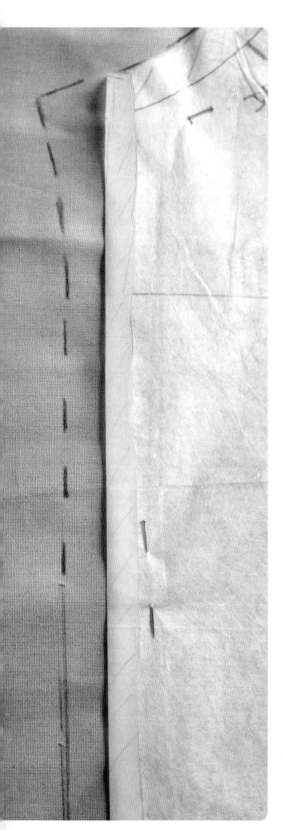

Once all the pattern pieces have been transferred and cut out, they must be copied, or pinned, onto the fabric. In pattern books or sewing books, there are often cutting plans that help us place the pieces correctly so too much fabric isn't wasted.

Depending on the pieces of the pattern to be cut (size, piece to be cut at the fold, on the bias, double ...), you may fold your fabric or you may not.

Always remember to have the wrong side of the fabric facing you. To correctly position your pattern on the fabric, locate the straight grain. Each pattern piece should have a double arrow showing you the straight edge. This is used to position the piece on your fabric.

Match the straight-grain markings on the paper pattern to the direction of the fabric to prevent the pieces from distorting over time. Even for reasons of fabric economy, it is strongly advised to not ignore the straight grain.

Be aware that the pattern motifs printed on your fabric are not necessarily reliable in positioning of your pattern in relation to the selvage. The lines or columns of patterns are not necessarily printed accurately, or even intentionally, horizontally/vertically on the fabric. Use your ruler to measure the distance from the double arrow on your pattern to the selvage of your material.

1. Position the pieces that lay on the fold first, then the rest of the pieces in order of size, from largest to smallest. Pin each piece with the points of the pins toward the inside of the pattern so you don't scratch yourself when handling them. More confident sewists can cut directly along the edge of the pattern. Less confident sewers can trace the outlines of the pieces with chalk or erasable marker.

2. For curved lines, use dotted lines; they are more accurate than following the entire curve.

▶ **Make a note of all the markings on the paper pattern. For the notches, you can use a small scissor cut perpendicular to the cut (maximum $\frac{3}{16}''$/0.5cm). You can also use the loop stitch, or tailor tack. With basting thread, sew into the mark on the pattern, taking the two layers of fabric together. When outlining a placement line, as for a pocket make loops at regular intervals. When the pattern is finished, gently pull the two layers of fabric apart and cut the thread between the two layers without cutting the fabric. There will be marks on both sides.**

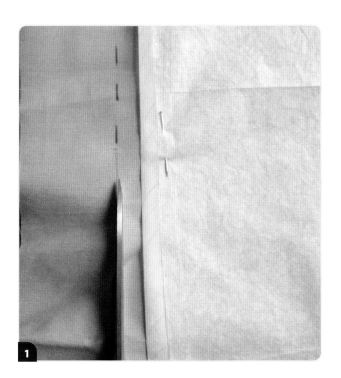

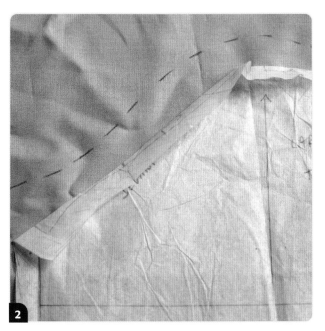

AAARGH!
I DON'T HAVE ENOUGH FABRIC

Check the reference height of the pattern: Most patterns are made for a height of 5´5˝ (168cm) or 5´6˝ (170cm). If you are 5´2˝ (160cm), you can shorten your pieces and save a few precious inches/centimeters of fabric. To do this, don't just cut off the bottom of your pattern pieces, but shorten the pattern at the horizontal line provided (see Some Modifications, page 60).

Another option is to combine two different fabrics. You can mix the fabrics within a piece or cut some pieces from another material.

MANAGING PATTERNED FABRIC

▸ The most important thing is to pin the pattern pieces noting where the notches along the seam lines are, as these help identify where garment pieces will be joined. You may have patterns to match horizontally (such as stripes), vertically, or in both directions (checks, for example). Take your time, the results will be worth it.

▸ However, be aware that the shape of a garment does not allow you to match patterns everywhere: Curves, darts, and gathers, for example, make some aspects of pattern matching impossible. It is even more difficult if your patterns are not well aligned on the straight grain (it happens). Grain always takes priority over the pattern matching.

1. Start by carefully folding your material front sides together, before pinning your pattern pieces. Match the patterns of the two layers of fabric. Pin along the selvage to ensure this alignment is not lost during the pinning, keeping the same distance between the fold and the selvage along the entire length of your fabric.

2. Pick a point to position your pattern pieces—always respecting the straight grain—and align them to the designs. For example, the bottom point of the armhole for a top or the notches on the sides for pants or skirts.

Then pin by aligning the pins to the patterns. You'll probably need to pin more than when you don't have to deal with patterned fabrics.

3. For fabric designs that allow it, place the edges of your pattern pieces between two lines/columns of the design to disguise complex seaming.

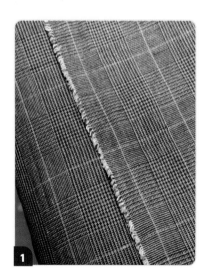

SEWING ON THE BIAS

Some patterns include sewing the fabric on the bias. This allows you to have garments that follow your shape and are, in fact, very comfortable.

To sew bias-cut pieces, you need to follow a few rules to simplify assembly and avoid curling seams:

Find the bias, the 45° line on the straight grain, by carefully aligning the arrow on the straight grain with the selvage.

Cut your pieces in one piece, not on the fold (so you can reconstruct a complete piece when you transfer your pattern).

Follow the cutting plan to the letter: Some pieces should not be cut side by side but head to tail so that they have the same orientation and drape similarly on the body.

Choose a suitable fabric, that is, one that is fluid enough to follow the curves of the body that the garment is supposed to follow.

Stabilize the curves (neckline and armholes in particular) with support seams (see The Support Seam, page 66).

Place your garment on a hanger for 24 hours before hemming to allow time for the fabric to find its final drape.

SEWING A MUSLIN

The muslin is the first version of a garment. It is sewn from a patterned (untreated) or non-precious fabric (old sheet or fabric-purchase error, for example). This "zero risk version" allows us to verify the construction instructions, the fall, and the overall volume of the garment; confirm the size and type of fabric chosen; and identify any adjustments necessary for your body.

▸ To check the fit and volume of the sewn piece, it is necessary to use a fabric in the test garment close to the one you will use (in terms of weight, elasticity, and fluidity) in the final garment. Be aware that there are several thicknesses of fabric available. Choose the one that is closest to your final fabric.

▸ Allow for a more significant seam allowance than a regular seam at least ¾″ (2cm) in case you need to add a few fractions of an inch or extra millimeters in certain places. Also, mark the chest, waist, and hip lines on your pattern pieces: They will allow you to check that they are well aligned with your body when you try them on.

▸ If there are any adjustments made during the fitting, write them down in marker on your fabric; then transfer them carefully to your paper pattern.

▸ **In a muslin, you don't usually do all the little details and finishing touches:** pockets, zippers, buttons, hems, and facings (unless you want to check the fit of one of these elements). Your fabric can be hand pieced or machine stitched with a longer stitch than usual (this allows you to go a little faster). Be sure to cut your pieces straight.

▸ Don't hesitate to reuse your muslin to sew new ones and make the most of this often maligned but beneficial exercise. Some sewists also use their muslin pieces as interfacing in their final project. You can also adopt the "wearable muslin" compromise: Use a piece of fabric for your muslin that you like enough to be sure you'll wear the finished garment, but not too precious in case this first version doesn't work out. Unlike a simple muslin, the wearable muslin requires you to do all the assembly and finishing. It is, therefore, a little more work than a muslin in the classical sense of the word.

CUTTING

Here is your fabric spread out on the table. Now you have to give it shape. Essential operation! This is not the time to tremble. Here's how to do it.

Suppose your fabric doesn't fit onto your cutting surface. In that case, you'll want to make sure the extra fabric is folded over (and not hanging over the edge of the counter), so it doesn't stretch the fabric and distort the measurements—especially when you're working with knits. When you're done cutting, the fabric that stretched under its own weight will return to its original size and you may end up with pieces that are smaller than expected.

▶ **Start the cut at the fold:** This eliminates the risk of catching only every other layer of fabric in your scissors.

▶ **Rotate the piece as you cut (this is easier than rotating around the piece). Make sure you are comfortable:** You should not be tense or cramped while cutting. If you are, you are not in the correct position. Make sure you choose scissors with a grip that fits your hand (in shape and size). Hold your scissors straight, let them glide across the table (don't lift the fabric to cut it: You'll distort it), and try to make "big bites" rather than small ones—the edges of your fabric will be cleaner.

▶ Once you've cut a piece, set it aside to avoid any untimely scissor cuts. Keep your patterns pinned to your pieces of fabric until you sew them; this avoids cold sweats afterward (while looking for the front/back side, identifying the center back and the side seam in a skirt piece, for example). Suppose you have a project with many pieces, similar front/back pieces, or a back side that is hard to distinguish from the front side. In that case, you can use tape (which is easy to write on) on the pattern pieces when you remove the pins. Write the name of the piece on the tape and apply it to the back side of the fabric so that you don't get confused when assembling.

▶ Once you've cut all your pieces, it's recommended that you save all of your fabric scraps until the end of your project. That way, you can test the setting of your machine before you start assembling your seams or have a little extra fabric in case of problems.

ASSEMBLING

Once the pattern pieces have been removed from the fabric (because they must be removed in time), they must be assembled. This consists of putting together the different pieces of the garment. The final success depends on the correct assembly of the various pieces. There are two assembly techniques: pinning and construction.

THE SUPPORT SEAM

Before assembling, it may be necessary to reinforce your pieces' curved or slanted edges to reduce the risk of distortion. This is especially true for necklines, armholes, and bias-cut parts of pieces (V-necks, for example), particularly if you work with a thin, flowing fabric.

To limit this risk, it is a good idea to machine stitch a line of straight stitches in the seam allowance, for example, 3/16″ (0.5cm) or 3/8″ (1cm) from the edge of the fabric, depending on the seam allowance provided in your pattern. Do this as you soon as you unpin the pattern from your fabric so that the piece does not have time to warp. Called stay stitching, this is not a construction seam although it is intended to stay in place permanently, done on one piece at a time in one layer, and is very useful to stabilize edges and prevent them from stretching during construction.

To stay stitch, use regular thread (the same as for the rest of the garment) and a needle that matches your fabric. However, choose a short stitch size $\frac{1}{16}''$ (1.5mm) or $\frac{1}{8}''$ (2mm), as tiny stitches are the most stabilizing. Do not stretch the fabric and stitch slowly, turning the fabric gently to keep the stitches even and parallel to the edge.

Stitch the supporting seams in opposite directions to ensure the symmetry of the shape: For a neckline, start from each shoulder and stitch towards the center (that is in two separate lines of stitching, rather than one around the whole neckline.

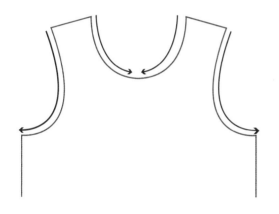

▸ **A habit to adopt.** The pattern instructions should indicate which support seams require two lines of stitching done towards the center front. However, this practice is often not mentioned. It's good practice though, so adopt the habit of doing it systematically on your necklines and all the lines in the bias if you use a fluid fabric.

▸ **Compare the piece to the pattern.** If in doubt, you can check that the fabric piece is the same as the pattern piece

(by overlapping) once you've stitched the support seam. If the fabric piece has stretched a little, lightly pull the thread every 3 stitches with a pin until the article looks like the pattern again.

PINNING

Pins are used to hold fabrics in place during assembly. Always start pinning on the ends, then on the assembly notches, then every $2\frac{3}{8}''$–$3\frac{1}{8}''$ (6–8cm). Do not pin from left to right, but always in sections (middle between two pins, new middle, and so on).

Be careful: In some materials, pins will leave holes that will not close. This is the case with leather or coated fabrics. Place your pins parallel to the edge of the fabric in the seam allowance (you will have to remove the pins as you sew). You can also use clips.

Always pin on the wrong side of the fabrics so that the pins are towards you when you machine stitch and the fabric flow is to your left. The more likely fabrics are to move (thin fabrics), the more necessary it is to pin with less space between two pins. Think about this before you start pinning so you don't have to undo everything and pin again ...

When stitching, it is recommended that you do not sew over the pins, removing them as you go along. Some people find that their machine will go over them without a problem, but with two conditions:

▸ **That the pins are pinned perpendicular to the seamline**

▸ **And that the heads of the pins protrude from the fabric so that they don't get trapped under the machine's foot**

Use flat-head pins, and be ruthless: Throw pins away as soon as they become a little twisted.

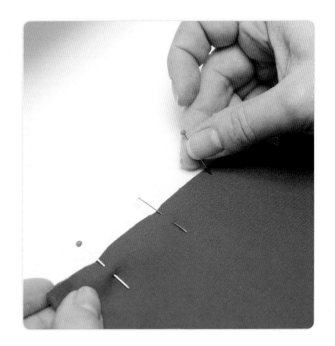

BASTING

Basting is the temporary joining of two layers of fabric with a long hand stitch—ideally within the seam allowances—in preparation for machine stitching. This ensures that the pieces will stay in position when machine sewed.

This step is used for delicate seams (rounded, multiple layers) when pinning is not enough, or for more involved details like zippers or pockets.

To make this stitch, you can use a particular thick cotton thread that breaks by hand so that it can be easily removed once the machine stitching is done; choose a contrasting color to see the thread well. If you don't have any basting thread on hand, you can use old spools of thread that have become too brittle to use as sewing thread.

The FIRST STITCHES
HAND STITCHING

THREADING A NEEDLE

Knowing how to thread a needle is the first step in sewing. Please note that you should never sew with a double thread, as it will get tangled.

1. Cut a thread about 12″ (30cm) long. Cut it cleanly. Beyond that, the thread may tangle when you sew. Hold it in your left hand and the needle in your right hand. Move the needle toward the thread (this is much easier). Pass the thread through the eye.

2. When sewing, hold the needle and thread simultaneously, pinching them between your thumb and forefinger to prevent the thread from slipping.

TIP

THE NEEDLE THREADER
You can also use a needle threader. It consists of a round piece of metal or plastic with a metal wire looped around it. Insert the metal loop into the eye of the needle, then the thread into the space formed by the loop. When you remove the loop, it pulls the thread through the eye.

3. Tie a knot at the end of the thread. To do this, make a loop around your finger. The knot shouldn't be too big, but it shouldn't pull through the fabric either. It should not be too far from the end of the thread so that it is not visible.

4. Rub your thumb and forefinger together. This will wrinkle the yarn, and the knot will form itself. Slide the knot onto the end of the thread. The knot is made, and the needle is ready.

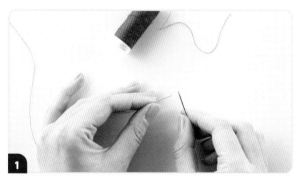

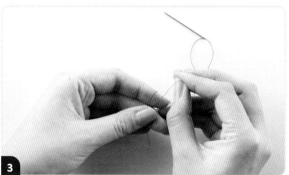

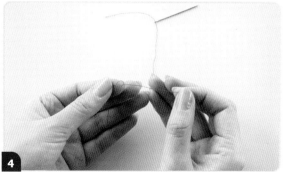

THE STRAIGHT STITCH

The straight stitch is the stitch you will use most frequently. It is a row of stitches forming a regular line of thread. It consists of passing over and under the fabric following a line—the more equal the distances between the stitches, the more regular and pretty the stitch. For a right-handed person, the stitch is done from right to left. For a left-handed person, it is done from left to right.

1. Hold the part to be sewn between the thumb and forefinger of one hand. The index finger is under the fabric, at the needle level. Place the needle on the underside side of the fabric and bring it through to the top side in the same motion.

2. Pull on the needle and thread. The knot will stop the thread.

3. About ⅛″ (3mm) further, stitch the needle from the top side to the back side of the fabric. Pull the thread through. Stitch, pull out, stitch, and pull out several times on the same point.

TIP
You can stitch in straight lines, curves, or right angles. Hand stitching offers a lot of flexibility.

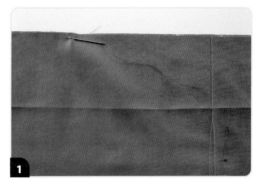

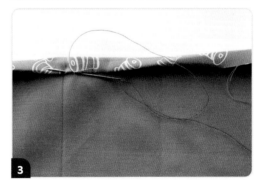

THE BACKSTITCH AND THE LOCKSTITCH

The backstitch is used to create a very secure seam. It can replace the stitch of the sewing machine. It creates a stronger seam than the straight stitch.

1. Place two pieces of fabric right sides together; then push the needle through one layer from the wrong side to hide the knot.

2. Bring the needle up through to the intended stitching line through all layers.

3. Take a stitch backwards down into the fabric, then bring the needle up further along the stitching line. Next take the needle down again into the hole of the previous stitch. Continue this way for the entire length advancing as you go. This technique essentially places stitches on top of each other, reinforcing each stitch.

4. Finish the seam by overlapping several stitches.

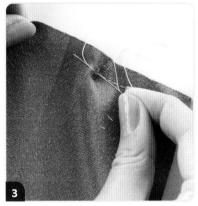
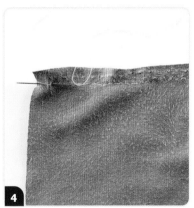

THE LOCKSTITCH

The lockstitch is similar to the backstitch. It is just as strong but quicker to make. It is performed like the backstitch, stitching precisely into the hole of the previous stitch. It is helpful for sewing areas that are not accessible to the machine. It is also used to stop a seam by overlapping a few stitches before cutting the thread or at the start of a seam to avoid making a knot. Choose short, thin needles.

THE SLIP STITCH

This stitch is used to sew two layers of fabric on the right side or to hem thin fabrics. This stitch is invisible.

1. Push the needle up from on the wrong side of the fabric, so the knot is hidden.

2. Take one small stitch in one layer of fabric then through the other layer.

3. Return the needle to the first layer of fabric, slipping the needle under the wrong side so the long thread between stitches is invisible, take a stitch and then take another stitch in the second layer of fabric.

4. Continue in this way then finish the seam by overlapping several stitches.

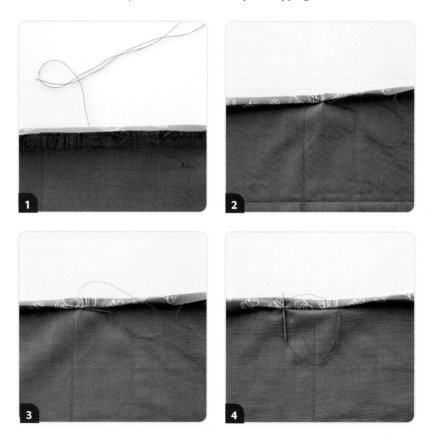

TIP

This is a reasonably loose seam: Don't pull the thread too tight.

THE CROSS-STITCH

This stitch is useful for quickly and easily attaching a detail like a small bow to the fabric.

1. Start stitching between the layers of fabric so the knot is hidden.

2. Pull the thread through all layers and stitch a few millimeters apart in a cross.

3. Stitch again over the first stitches through all layers.

4. Tie a knot, hiding it between the layers.

Whether straight, diagonal, or crossed, these other stitch types will help you tack, sew, and finish your seams beautifully.

THE BASTING OR TACKING STITCH

The basting stitch is an elongated straight stitch. It is used to temporarily join two pieces of fabric before creating a permanent seam. It is used for slippery fabrics, curves, or when precision sewing is required.

▸ Thread your needle with a thread that contrasts with the fabric. Do not tie a knot at the end of the thread. Stitch the needle into the material at the intended seam location. Stitch the thread and needle together about ⅝″ (1.5cm) apart, taking all the layers. Continue along the entire length. Stitch the final seam; then pull one end of the thread to remove the basting threads.

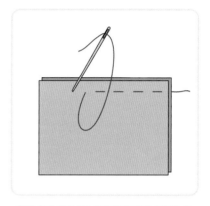

THE OVERLOCK STITCH

If a fabric is too thick to do a traditional stitch, the overlock stitch is ideal for joining the two edges.

▸ Tie a knot at the end of your thread, then stitch evenly from left to right, straddling the edges of the fabrics. Use tiny stitches to achieve a strong finish. Finish with a knot.

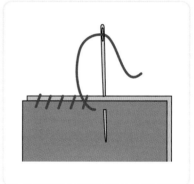

THE OVERCAST STITCH

This stitch prevents the cut edges of an open seam from fraying. It is created with over and under stitches on each edge for thick fabrics and by taking the two edges together for thin materials. It is similar to the overlock stitch. The overcast stitch is recognized as seam finish with a series of stitches straddling the raw edge of the fabric.

▸ Hold the fabric so the edge being overcast is not towards you. Place the needle between ⅛″ (3mm) and ¼″ (6mm) from the edge, pass the thread over it to make a stitch almost perpendicular to the edge, and repeat next to it. Do not overstretch the thread.

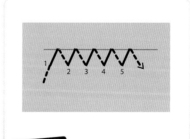

TIP
If the fabric frays, make the stitches closer together.

THE BUTTONHOLE STITCH

This stitch is used to hand stitch buttonholes or to attach fasteners.

▸ Sew around the edge of the fabric without leaving any space between the stitches. Make the stitches from right to left, pushing the needle from the edge to the inside of the fabric. Then pass the needle through the loop formed by the thread at the edge of the work as it passes through the fabric and again as it exits the fabric. Finish by tying a knot.

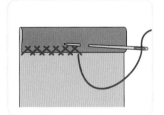

THE HEM STITCH

This stitch is used to create hems that are invisible on the outside of the fabric. It is ideal for pants or tailored skirts.

▸ Make a hem on the fabric, folding the material twice to the wrong side. Tie a knot at the end of the thread, and stitch through the inner fold. Grab 1 or 2 threads from the main fabric of your work; then slip the needle at an angle through the hemline. Finish by tying a knot.

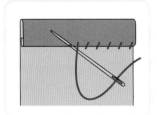

THE STOCKING STITCH

It is used to hem thick fabrics or to join two fabrics.

> **TIP**
> This stitch is not hidden and can be used for decorative purposes.

▸ It is sewn from left to right. You may or may not tuck in the hem. Take the needle out, and stitch higher up and to the right. Stitch at the bottom left to cross the threads.

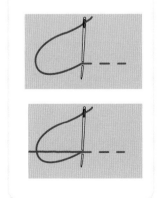

THE SATIN STITCH

This is a decorative stitch. You can also use it to attach appliqués or make buttonholes.

▸ Make a knot at the end of your thread; then create straight stitches on the line where you want to make your satin stitches. They can be done either from left to right or right to left. At the end of the design, create a perpendicular stitch to the design. (Stitch just above the last straight stitch, and pull the needle out from underneath, near the previous straight stitch.)

▸ Repeat along the length of the line, bringing the stitches as close together as possible so that the fabric is not visible between them.

The
FIRST STITCHES
MACHINE STITCHING

Machines offer several types of stitches suitable for certain kinds of sewing.

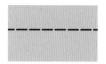

THE STRAIGHT STITCH

▸ This is the basic stitch you will use for machine stitching.

THE ZIGZAG STITCH

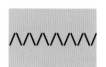

▸ It is widely used for overcasting, decorative stitching, or strengthening seams.

▸ The presser foot for the zigzag stitch can be the same as the presser foot for the straight stitch, as long as the needle can move from left to right.

▸ Set the machine settings to the zigzag stitch. A larger zigzag can be used to finish or make strong seams.

THE TIGHT ZIGZAG STITCH

▸ It is very often used to sew appliqués.

▸ If you set the stitch length very short, you will make a close, covered, embroidery stitch.

THE ZIGZAG STITCH (OVERCASTING)

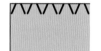

▸ This stitch prevents the fabric from fraying and allows you to sew elastic fabrics if you don't have a serger (you can also use it to attach appliqués).

▸ Place the edge of the fabric under the presser foot. The needle should swing in and out of the fabric side to side. You can use this stitch to overcast one layer or two layers at a time.

THE OVEREDGE ZIGZAG STITCH (MULTI-STEP)

It is ideal for sewing elastics.

THE BUTTONHOLE STITCH

It is made in four steps on the most standard machines, and automatically on the most sophisticated, but its function remains the same. Learn to use the dials or settings on your machine to make the broadest range of buttonhole types.

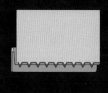

THE HEM STITCH

It will help you make invisible hems faster than by hand.

TRIPLE STRAIGHT OR ZIGZAG STITCHES

They reinforce the seams made.

THE OVERLOCK OR OVEREDGE STITCH

It allows you to make beautiful finishes resembling those of the serger.

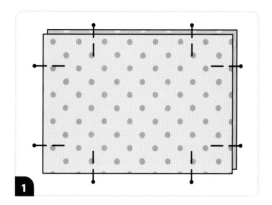

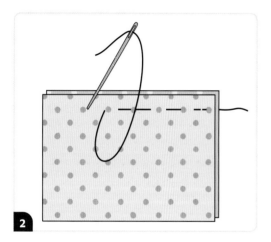

Starting A SEAM

MAKING THE FIRST SEAM BY HAND

Lay the fabrics to be joined, right sides together, on a large table to get comfortable. Trim the edges and corners.

1. Pin the fabrics together. This will hold the two layers of fabric together. Insert the pins perpendicular to the seamline. This way, you can remove them easily, and you won't get pricked while sewing.

2. Baste at the intended seam location, taking all layers together.

3 & 4. Make your seam using a thread that is slightly darker than the fabric. Tie a knot at the end of the thread, or start your seam with overlapping stitches. To finish the seam, tie a knot or layer the stitches; then cut the remaining thread.

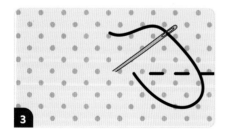

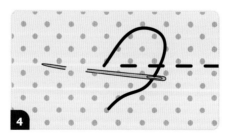

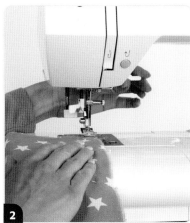

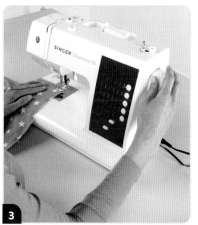

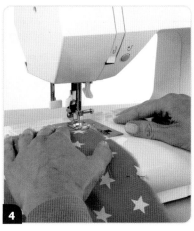

MAKING THE FIRST SEAM BY MACHINE

Straight stitching is the basis of machine sewing and the first stitch that existed on mechanical machines. With this just this one stitch you can already sew any straight seams and is the only stitch you need to make such items as cushions, covers, or bags.

1. Place the fabric under the machine's presser foot, parallel to the seam marks. If the seam allowance is ³⁄₁₆″ (0.5cm), lay the fabric along the ³⁄₁₆″ (0.5cm) mark. If the seam is ³⁄₈″ (1cm), lay the fabric along the ³⁄₈″ (1cm) mark.

2. Lower the presser foot gently to avoid damaging the machine or moving the fabric.

3. Turn the handwheel to insert the needle into the fabric.

4. Start sewing. Place your hand on the side; it should not pull the fabric. The left hand at the back is only guiding the material.

SEWING STRAIGHT

Several things can help you:

› Sew slowly. With practice, you will be able to sew faster and faster while remaining accurate.

› Draw lines on the fabric and follow them.

› Buy a foot that guides the fabric or a magnetic fabric guide to hold the fabric in place.

› Stitch using the lines engraved on the throat plate as a guide. These seam markers allow you to stitch evenly and get the desired seam shape. This requires a regular and precise cut of the fabrics beforehand. Some projects require a large seam allowance: Stick masking tape at the desired measurement if you don't have a corresponding marker on the throat plate.

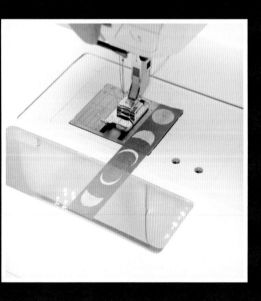

SEWING SEVERAL LAYERS OF FABRIC

If you are sewing several layers together you need to know how to keep the fabrics in place.

1. Layer the different pieces of fabric. Pin; then baste the pieces and remove the pins (you can use thins silk pins that don't get caught in the presser foot).

2. Stitch at ³⁄₁₆″ (0.5cm), the width of a presser foot.

TIP

If the fabrics are thick and you can't start sewing, it may be because the presser foot is tilted. In this case:

▸ Take a piece of fabric and fold it to be the same thickness as the fabrics you are sewing.

▸ Place it halfway on your presser foot before the needle, stuck to the fabrics ready to be sewn.

▸ The feed dogs can move forward and push this fabric "shim" toward the back of the machine. It will not be sewn.

SEWING CORNERS

Many projects require angled seams. Stitching an angle without stopping at the seam is not very difficult, although you must take care to get a clean angle.

1. Stitch to within ³⁄₁₆″ (0.5cm) of the edge for a ³⁄₁₆″ (0.5cm) seam. Upon reaching the corner, lower the needle into the fabric, lift the presser foot, and turn the fabric 90° to align the second side facing you.

2. Lower the presser foot. Resume sewing on the other side.

3. When finished sewing, trim the right angles on the bias a few millimeters or fractions of an inch from the seam.

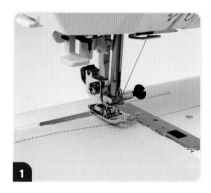

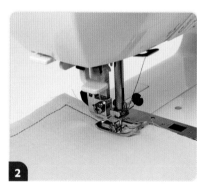

SEWING CORNERS IN VERY THICK FABRICS

Sometimes it isn't easy to make a clean angle. For very thick fabrics, you need to sew a diagonal stitches across the corners. This will allow you to turn the fabric right side out after notching the corner.

SEWING A CORNER OF A DIFFERENT SIZE

Sew along the seam allowance. Stop the seam, lower the needle, raise the presser foot, rotate the fabrics, lower the presser foot, and continue sewing.

SEWING CURVES

Whether your curve is concave or convex, the edges of the fabric should remain aligned with your seam allowance mark on the right side of the presser foot. Slowly rotate your work as you sew.

Experiment with the presser foot to achieve a successfully curved seam and turn the fabric as you go. Stitch gently to avoid "beaks" once the work is turned right side out!

If you find yourself stitching away from the seam guide, stick your needle into the fabric with the machine's handwheel (always turning towards you), raise the presser foot and move your work back towards the seam allowance marking, then lower your presser foot and restitch.

Once the sewing is finished, stay on the wrong side and:

▸ Notch the seam allowance for convex seams. Cut small V's in the seam allowance.

▸ Notch the excess seam allowance if you have a concave seam.

This will allow the fabric to sit correctly without creating unsightly layers or folds, and to fit the curve. Do this with small embroidery scissors so as not to cut your seam.

Then turn your work right side out, shape your curve by hand, and iron.

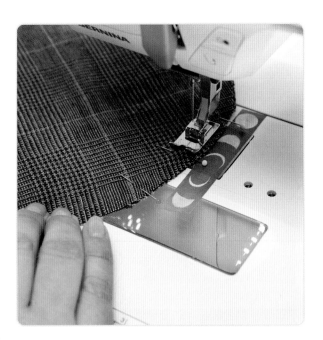

TIP

To achieve an even seamline, slow down before the curve, while gently guiding the fabric so that the edges remain aligned with the throat plate markings. When stitching a curve, it is even more important to focus on the throat plate markings and forget about the needle.

Stopping A SEAM

MAKE A KNOT BY HAND

1. Cut the threads. You can use the notch behind the presser foot or a pair of scissors.

2. Pull the top thread (the on the upper spool) slightly, release the bobbin thread with a pin, and knot the two threads together.

BACKSTITCH ON THE MACHINE

1. At the beginning of the seam, make a straight stitch for ⅜″ (1cm); then engage the reverse gear and stitch in the backstitch for ⅜″ (1cm), picking up on the initial seam. Start again in straight stitch. At the end of the seam, set the machine to backstitch; then backstitch ⅜″ (1cm).

2. Raise the needle and presser foot, and gently pull your work.

TIP

For machines that do not backstitch, rotate the fabric 180°, stitch in the straight stitch, and rotate 180° again to bring the fabric back to the right direction. Be careful; this is only possible with thin fabrics in small lengths.

Both methods have their advantages. Sewing over the original seam with a backstitch is faster. The stitching is more substantial, but the seam stop is visible, especially on hems. Tying a knot is longer; recutting the threads is tricky because if you cut too close to the knot, it can come undone. But the seam stop is not visible afterward.

When you cut the threads, always leave a few inches of thread. If you cut the threads flush with the needle or bobbin, you must rethread them on the next seam.

Finishing
A SEAM

OVERCASTING

Some fabrics need to be overcast. If you don't overcast them, the material will fray to the seam, and the stitching will eventually come loose. You can overcast before or after assembly.

OVERCASTING BY HAND

1. Stitch a thread on the wrong side of one of the layers; then stitch on the wrong side ⅛″ (3mm) or 3/16″ (4mm) further. This way, the thread will straddle the edge.

2. Stitch the second layer the same way.

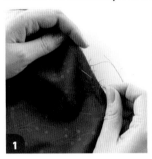 

OVERCASTING BY MACHINE

1. Set the machine to a medium-size zigzag stitch. Place the presser foot flush with the edge of the fabrics. Insert the needle. Stitch along the edge of the fabric.

NOTCHING

This step is essential when working on pieces with corners and curves.

After sewing and before turning the work right side out, it is necessary to notch to avoid creases.

Using scissors, make small triangular cuts spaced evenly from the edge of the fabric without going all the way to the seam. If the material is thin, cut simple slits.

PRESSING SEAMS

At the end of each seam, always press—either to one side or open.

When it says, "press open," separate the seam allowances with the iron by flattening them on either side of the seam. This allows the seam to be as flat as possible and avoids fabric overhang when assembling a garment.

The Different FINISHES

SEWING A SEAM CLOSED

The hidden stitch is helpful for making an invisible seam and a neat finish on a pant leg or a sleeve bottom, for example. It is also used to close an opening on a seam that has been used to turn a work right side out.

BY HAND

1. To make a discreet hand stitch, choose a thread that matches the dominant color of your fabric. Do not tie a knot in your thread; instead, start with several stitches in place, leaving only a small amount of thread hanging out, then work through your loops 2 to 3 times to form knots. Fold the edges of the fabrics from the right side inward, and iron a ⅜″ (1cm) hem (seam allowance). Position the hems together, edge to edge, and pin the layers together. Sew the first stitch from the inside of the hem onto the fold to hide the thread knot. Sew the second stitch into the fold of the

other hem, working backwards and forwards. Sew the third stitch into the fold of the first hem and continue to join the two hems. The closer your stitches are, the finer and more discreet the seam.

2. When you reach the end of the seam, pass your thread through a small loop several times and then pull it tight to lock your seam. Then cut your thread flush with the fabric.

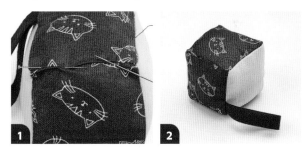

BY MACHINE

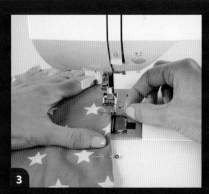

1. If the seam allowance is ⅜″ (1cm), fold the edges inward. Press, pin, and baste.

3. If you don't want to baste but sew directly, remove the pins as you go, just before sewing.

TOPSTITCHING

Topstitching is a reinforcing or decorative seam. It can be single, double or triple, and so on.

SIMPLE TOPSTITCHING

The simple topstitch is made close to the seamline. If you have folded your seam allowances to the right of your seam line, as in a flat felled seam for example, on the front side stitch a new line at ⅛″ (0.3cm) from the construction stitch line.

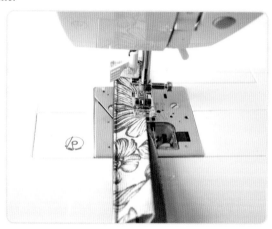

THE EDGE STITCH

An edge topstitch is used to fold over a facing, or band, by stitching very close to the garment seam.

The part underneath remains well hidden inside the garment. All seam thicknesses must be taken with the topstitch.

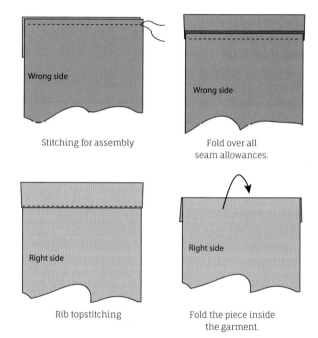

Stitching for assembly   Fold over all
                                seam allowances.

Rib topstitching   Fold the piece inside
                          the garment.

THE BIAS

MAKING BIAS STRIPS

You can find ready-made bias strips in sewing and craft stores, but you can also make bias strips yourself with a chosen fabric.

1. Fold a square of fabric diagonally. From this diagonal, draw one or more parallel strips, spaced 1⅝″ (4cm) apart for a finished bias of ⅜″ (1cm).

2. Cut them along the lines. You get beveled strips.

3. Once you have the desired length, sew the strip's front sides together to form one strip. Press the seam open.

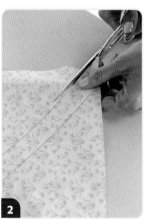

TIPS

The width of the bias strip depends entirely on the purpose. For example, there are very thin bias strips ⅜″ (1cm) wide (plus folded edges) and others that can be up to 4″ (10cm) wide (plus folded edges) for quilting borders.

Cutting strips on the bias may seem absurd in terms of fabric savings, especially if you choose expensive fabrics. But it is essential to gain the flexibility necessary to go around some edges.

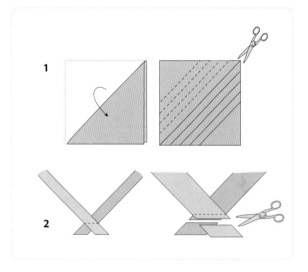

APPLYING BIAS STRIPS

Bias strips cleanly finish the edges or the inside of a garment. They are flexible and can withstand slight distortion, allowing them to be sewn onto different pieces. They can be used as a seam allowance or as a facing around a cutout.

BY HAND

1. Unfold the bias strip. Lay it right sides together, following the edge of the fabric. Match the edges.

2. Sew the seam in the flap with the straight stitch.

3. Fold the bias tape over to the wrong side of the fabric and slipstitch the flap to the wrong side.

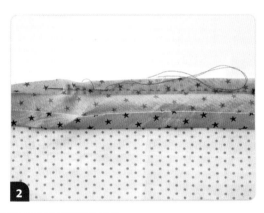
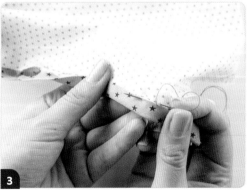

USING THE MACHINE

1. Unfold the bias strip. Place it right side down on the right side of the fabric's edge. Baste, then stitch the bias into the fold.

2. Fold the bias strip to the other side of the fabric. Fold inward. Machine stitch on the bias.

3. For more finesse, you can finish the bias stitching by hand. Fold over the bias to the other side of the fabric. Fold inward. Stitch the bias to the fabric with small slip stitches.

TIP

Since bias is used to trim edges, do not overcast where you will be placing it.

APPLY BIAS IN ONE MACHINE SEAM

Slide the folded bias over the edge of the fabric. Pin perpendicular to the edge.

Baste the entire bias to hold it to the fabric: It tends to slip when passing under the presser foot. Stitch in one seam, taking both bias layers into the seam.

Make a slight tuck of ³⁄₁₆″ (0.5cm) on the upper bias. Overlap the ends to close before sewing.

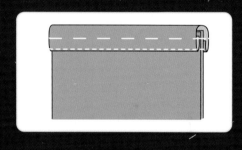
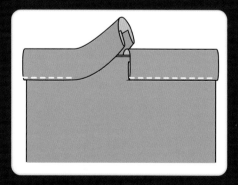

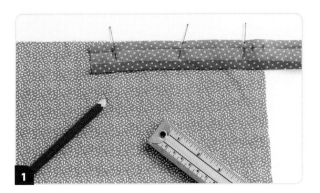

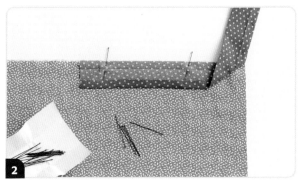

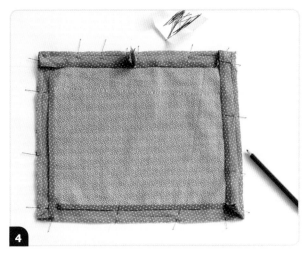

APPLY BIAS ON A CORNER

1. Pin the bias strip edge to edge and right sides together on the fabric, leaving ¾″ (2cm) extra for finishing, and mark a point ⅓″ (8mm) from the edge.

2. Fold the bias up to mark a diagonal line through the point.

3. Place the bias on the edge of the fabric, right sides together. A fold will form. Mark a point that matches the first point. Pin the bias all the way around.

4. Stitch the bias by stopping the machine before the fold with a locking stitch. Pick up the stitching after the fold.

5. Fold the fabric in half and stitch the extra ¾″ (2cm) of bias from the beginning.

6. Fold the bias to the other side using the iron.

7. Pin the corners nicely using the tip of your scissors to get a perfect angle.

8. Stitch flush around the bias.

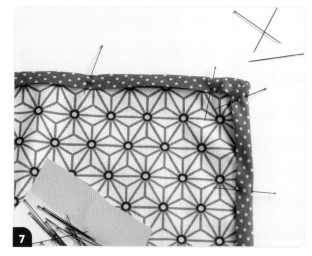

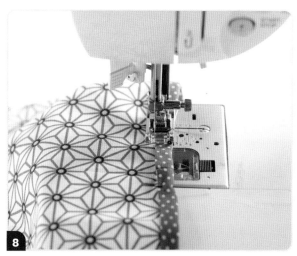

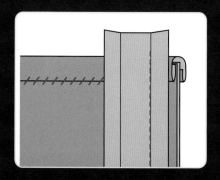

LAYERED CORNERS

Cut the bias strips flush with the fabric. Lay down the bias strips side by side. Start with opposite sides.

Lay the other two bias strips over the corners. Stitch the bias open on one side.

With the help of the other edges, tuck in each end ³⁄₁₆″ (0.5cm). Fold over the bias and sew along the entire length.

FRENCH SEAMS

This finish is suitable for fine and light fabrics (cotton batiste, cotton voile, and viscose). It should be avoided on materials that are too thick and not suitable for rounded seams.

It consists of two straight lines of stitching that enclose the edges of the fabric, preventing it from fraying.

BY HAND

1. Lay the two layers of fabric wrong sides together.

2. Sew with a straight stitch ⅜″ (1cm) from the edge.

3. Trim the seam allowance to ³⁄₁₆″ (0.5cm).

4. Turn fabrics right sides together. Press. Sew ⅜″ (1cm) again from the edge. This will hide the first seam.

BY MACHINE

To make a French seam, it is necessary to proceed in two steps. We will assume that the seam allowance is ⅝″ (1.5cm).

1. Pin your fabrics wrong sides together, and straight stitch ³⁄₁₆″ (0.5cm) from the edge. Turn your work inside out and press the seam. Trim any tiny threads that stick out; then trim the seam allowance to within ⅛″ (2 to 3mm) of the seam.

2. Pin the fabrics together again, but this time right sides together. Straight stitch ⅜″ (1cm) from the edge. Trim any tiny threads that stick out. Open the seam and iron the fabric flap on the back. The first seam is encased and hidden in the second.

3. For a stylish effect, you can make a reverse French seam, meaning the fabric flap will be on the outside, not the inside.

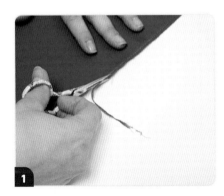

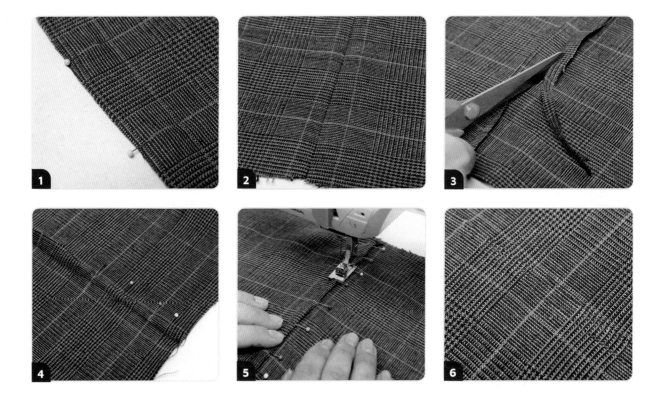

FOLDED SEAMS

This solid finish is suitable for all fabrics, including thicker ones like denim.

However, it requires a large enough seam allowance to be made (ideally ¾"/2cm). Note that a stitch line will be visible on the right side of your garment with this finish.

1. Make a simple first assembly seam.

2. Press your seam allowances to one side (it doesn't matter which one).

3. Trim the bottom margin so that it is reduced by half.

4. Fold down the top seam allowance to cover the bottom seam allowance.

5. Press to secure. Pin and stitch right sides together, a few millimeters from your original joining seam.

6. The stitch line is visible on the right side.

PIPED SEAMS

Piping is made with the fabric's bias and may or may not be furnished with a cord. It is caught in a seam so that it forms a regular fold on the front side of the work. It can be used for two purposes: It can be used to edge a collar, a pocket, cuffs, or a belt, but it can also reinforce a work.

PREPARE THE PIPING

1. Draw a straight line at 45° to the edge of the fabric. Cut on the bias of the fabric.

2. Cut a second straight line 2⅜″ (6cm) apart (for a thin cord) with a mark.

3. Fold the fabric in half lengthwise. Place the cord in the center of the bias. Pin in place.

4. Baste the cord to hold it in place.

5. Change the presser foot on the machine. Install a special piping presser foot or a zipper presser foot. Stitch close to the edge of the piping.

TIP

Don't buy too large a cord, especially if the piping is placed in an area subject to wear. Always wash your cord before covering it to prevent shrinkage later.

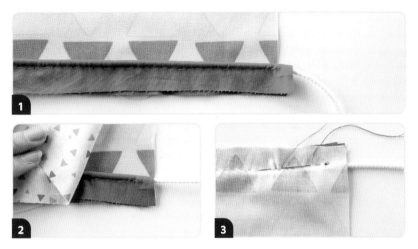

SEWING PIPING BY HAND

1. Place the piping on the right side of a fabric layer, with the cord facing inward. Baste; then sew the piping in place with the straight stitch.

2. Place the second layer of fabric on top of the first, right sides together. The piping will be between the layers.

3. Stitch over the previous seam; then turn right side out.

STITCHING PIPING

1. Pin the piping to the right side of the fabric, with the cord facing inward. Place your pins lengthwise and upside down.

2. If you want to place piping in a corner or a curve, notch the fabric to avoid pulling.

3. To finish neatly, cross and overlap the two ends of the piping.

4. Baste the piping to keep it in place.

Change your presser foot to the zipper foot. Set up your foot so that your needle is above the piping seam. Stitch the piping ⅜″ (1cm) from the edge. Place the two layers of fabric right sides together. The piping is inserted between the two layers. Stitch on all sides over the first seam allowance. Leave 2″ to 4″ (5cm to 10cm) of opening to turn over. Turn tright side out. Bring out the corners. Close the opening with small invisible stitches.

TIP

If you are piping a piece of work, do not start at a corner: You will have a lot of trouble connecting the two ends. Leave a length of piping free at the beginning and end. When you join the ends, cut the cord to the exact size and hand sew the two ends together, after folding them over with a few stitches where they meet. Finish threading the piping into place.

COLLARS

SEWING A NECKLINE INSERT

Sewing a neckline insert allows you to make a charming neckline without sewing a collar or bias binding.

1. Place the larger neckband on a flat surface, right side up. Place the side shirtings on top of the larger shirting, front sides together. Match the short lengths. Machine stitch the short sides.

2. Place the garment on a flat surface, right side facing you. Lay the neckline insert on top, wrong side facing you. Match the edges. Pin evenly. Machine stitch ³⁄₁₆″ (0.5cm) from the edge.

3. Clip the entire neckline evenly. Cut small triangles with your scissors to remove thickness from the fabric. (Be careful not to cut the seam!) This will make it easier to turn and shape the insert.

4. Turn the garment over to the back side. Press to set the neckline insert well, and hold with a small slip stitch at the shoulder seams.

SEWING A SIMPLE COLLAR WITHOUT A COLLAR STAND

You may need to stitch a collar to finish the top of a garment.

1. Join the two collar layers, right sides together. Stitch the entire rounded edge ³⁄₁₆″ (0.5cm) from the edge.

2. Fold the collar in half to determine its center. Place a marker pin in the middle. Place a marker pin in the middle of the back of the garment. Place the collar on the neckline, right sides together, and match the center pins. Pin the collar to the neckline, right sides together. Pinning allows the collar to sit as well as possible.

3. Place the facing on top, right side against the collar. The collar is now inserted between the garment and the facing. Pin, then baste. Stitch the neckline, collar, and facing to the entire neckline of the garment in one seam. Remove the basting thread. Clip the rounded edges.

4. Turn the facing to the wrong side of the garment. Press to hold the facing in place.

SEWING A ROUND COLLAR WITH A CUTOUT

This collar is in two parts that must fit together. It is a lovely finishing touch to a tunic.

1. Place the two collars right sides together. Pin or baste to hold the whole rounded edge in place (see photo, below). Stitch the whole rounded edge. Leave the flat part (that is to be sewn to the shirt) unstitched. Clip to remove thickness from the fabric along the sewn seam so you can turn it inside out.

Turn the collar right side out and press.

2. From the fabric's bias, cut a strip 6″ × the notch length. Place the strip on the notch, right sides together. Pin along both sides of the notch (see photo, below).

Stitch the strip to the shirt. Fold in the long unsewn edge. Fold the strip over and sew it as you would a bias strip.

3. Place the garment on a flat surface, right side up. Fold the collar in half to determine its center. Place a center marker pin. Fold the back in half. Place a marker pin. Place the collar on the back, right sides together and matching the center markings. Pin one collar layer to the neckline and stitch that collar layer to the shirt.

4. Fold in ³⁄₁₆″ (0.5cm) on the unstitched layer of the collar. Fold this collar to the inside of the shirt. Stitch the collar to the inside of the shirt with small slip stitches.

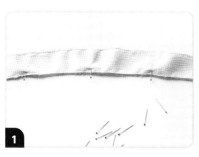

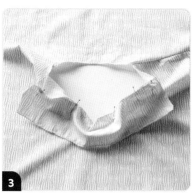

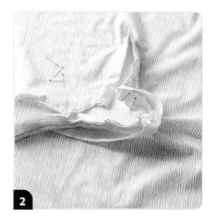

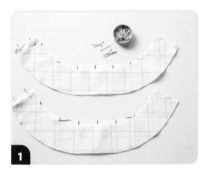

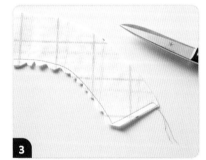

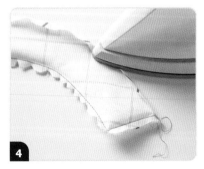

SEWING A YOKE COLLAR

This collar is unique, as it goes on a top or dress without shoulders.

1. After cutting the four collar pieces, join the pieces two at a time, front to back and right sides together. Assemble the collar and collar lining in this way. Press open the seams.

2. Place both collars right sides together. Join, then stitch the inner edge and short ends together, leaving open the outer edge.

3. Clip the seam allowances. This step is essential. Removing a little fabric thickness allows you to turn the collar inside out very neatly.

4. Prepare the outer collar. Press a ³⁄₁₆″ (0.5cm) seam to the wrong side of the collar on the long side. Turn the collar right side out. Press to hold the collar in place. Open the collar. Slide the top of the garment into the collar. Baste the collar to hold the layers in place. Stitch the collar to the top of the garment with a slip stitch. Sew around the entire collar.

This collar is made in a jersey fabric. You can use a serger or the zigzag stitch on your sewing machine to stitch it.

1. Close the collar band by pinning the short sides front sides together and stitching ³⁄₁₆″ (0.5cm) from the edge. This will create a ring.

2. Fold the back sides together and press the ring, forming the funnel neckband.

3. Place the collar band against the neckline of the garment, front sides together and edge to edge. Pin the seam of the collar band to the right shoulder seam. Then fold the band in half and continuing pinning around the neck, including over the left shoulder seam.

4. Sew the collar band to the neckline of the garment ³⁄₁₆″ (0.5cm) from the edges using a serger or sewing machine.

5. Iron.

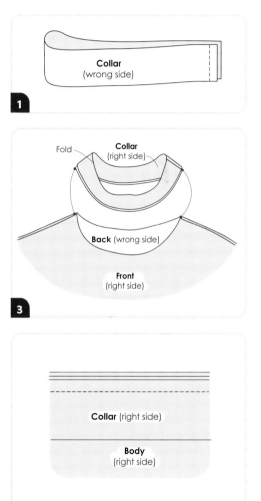

1
Collar (wrong side)

3
Fold
Collar (right side)
Back (wrong side)
Front (right side)

4
Collar (right side)
Body (right side)

SEWING A COLLAR WITH A BRAID OR PIPING

Adding a fancy braid to a seam can add color and give a design some pizzazz.

1. Baste the fancy braid or piping to the front side of a collar strip raw edges even. Turn the scallop to the inside of the fabric. Machine stitch the braid or piping on the flat part of the braid/piping.

2. Place the second collar layer on top. The braid will be sandwiched between the two layers of fabric. Pin and then evenly baste the collar and the braid together to hold them in place.

3. Stitch along the line of the first seam. The secret to successful braid application is to place the second row of stitches over the first. Remove the basting thread.

4. Turn the collar front side out. As you turn it over, the braid will flip out. Iron to make neat finish.

5. Fold in ³⁄₁₆″ (0.5 cm) on each unstitched side. Place the collar strip on the neckline, overlapping the back's middle with the strip's middle seam, right sides together. Stitch the collar ³⁄₁₆″ (0.5 cm) from the edge. Press.

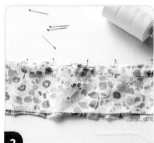

APPLYING HIDDEN BIAS TO A NECKLINE

Bias can be used to finish a neckline neatly.

1. Place the bias binding right sides together with the neckline. Pin by pulling gently on the bias to fit the rounded shape of the neckline. Trim the excess.

2. Stitch the bias placing the stitches in slightly above the fold line you will see along the bias. Make notches in the curves with scissors to help the bias fold properly.

3. Turn the bias over the neckline. Press it well with an iron.

4. Fold the bias again towards the inside of the garment. This may appear to lift the neckline slightly, so press well and pin to hold the bias in place.

5. Topstitch at the edge of the bias, taking care not to catch the fabric and make a fold.

6. You have applied a hidden bias. Your neckline is clean, and your bias is invisible on the garment.

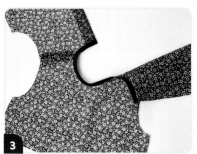

ATTENTION

It turns a lot! The pinning must follow the neckline to avoid folds.

SEWING A COLLAR WITH A COLLAR STAND

Traditionally, adding a stand to a collar gave it height and made it possible to wear a jacket.

1. Prepare the collar by placing the two collar layers right sides together, edges even. Stitch ³⁄₁₆″ (0.5cm) from the edge (leaving the edge that will attach to the collar stand unstitched).

2. Clip the corners.

3. After turning the collar right side out and pressing it well, place a collar stand on each side of the collar right sides together, long edges even. The two collar stands are then right sides together, the collar sandwiched between them. Pin or baste to secure the collar stands. Machine stitch the collar stands along around the curves and along the collar edge. Leave the neckline edge unstitched.

4. Turn the collar stand right side out. Press to give it a clean shape around the seams. Pressing will smooth out any small imperfections in the details. Additionally, a well-pressed collar makes the rest of construction easier.

5. Find the center of the collar stand. Mark the center of the collar with a pin. Find the center of the neckline and mark with a second pin. Place the collar stand on the shirt's neckline right sides together matching the center marks. Pin evenly.

6. Cut a strip of fabric from the bias 1⅝″ (4cm) wide × the length of the collar stand (you can buy bias tape from sewing and craft stores). Place the strip on the neckline over the collar stand.

Baste the neckline, collar stand, and bias tape to hold the layers in place. Then machine stitch and remove the basting thread.

7. Fold the bias tape over the collar stand seam to the wrong side of the fabric, inside the neckline of the shirt. Turn under the raw edge of the bias and sew by hand to cover and hide the seam of the collar stand.

8. Fold the shirt's facing or so it covers the collar stand's end and bias tape and hand stitch the top of the band in place along the neckline seam. This will make the collar very neat. Press.

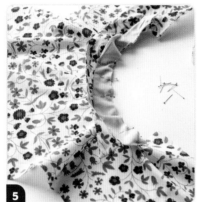

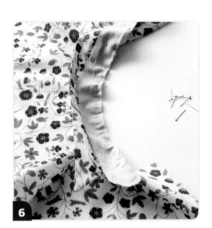

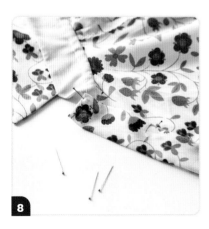

SLEEVES

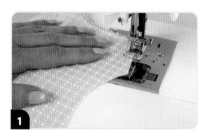

Assembling the shoulder of a garment is relatively easy. Follow the rules of cutting and assembly, and the sewing will be a breeze.

1. Overcast, or serge finish, the garment pieces.

2. Join the back to the front at the shoulders. Pin in place.

3. Stitch ³⁄₁₆″ (0.5cm) from the edge.

4. Press the seam open.

After the shoulders are sewn the sleeves are next. There are different ways to attach a sleeve. This one is relatively quick, especially for light cotton tunics.

1. Run a gathering stitch through the top of the sleeve. Gathering marks are often given on patterns and should be transferred to the fabric.

The sleeve is always wider than the armhole to allow the arm to move. It is necessary to reduce the sleeve's width to fit the armhole.

2. Place each sleeve on an armhole, front sides together. Pin the ungathered part to the armhole.

Then pull the gathering threads to distribute the gathers from the top of

the sleeve, adjusting the sleeve length to that of the arm hole, and pin in place. Baste the sleeve in place. Stitch. Remove the gathering threads.

3. Stitch the sleeve and the side in a single seam, from the cuff to the bottom of the tunic.

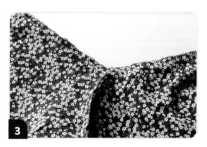

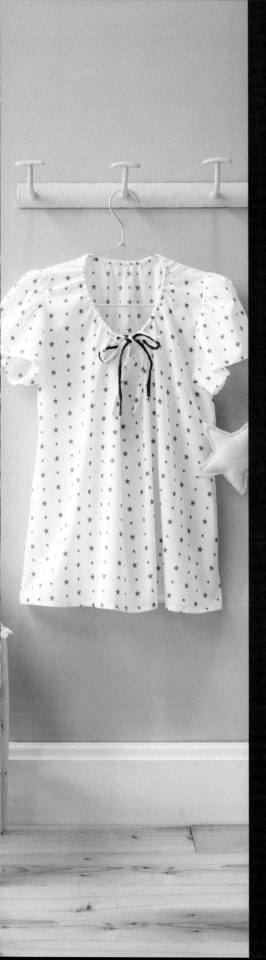

SEWING A GATHERED SLEEVE

Some sleeves are barely gathered or pleated, while others play with this difference in volume.

1. Transfer the gather marks provided on the sleeve pattern. Pin the sleeve seams together and stitch.

2. Make gathering stitches between the markings as indicated by the pattern.

3. Turn the sleeve right side out. The garment is still left inside out; do not turn it after sewing the shoulder and side seams. Slide the sleeve into the garment. The sleeve and garment are now right sides together. Match the raw edges of the sleeve armhole and the portion of the sleeve below the gathering stitches.

4. Pin the entire bottom of the sleeve, below the gathering stitches, into the armhole. Then working on the top part of the sleeve pull on the gathering threads so that the diameter of the sleeve matches the armhole perfectly. Pin in place. Stitch the sleeve into the armhole. Remove the gathering threads and pins.

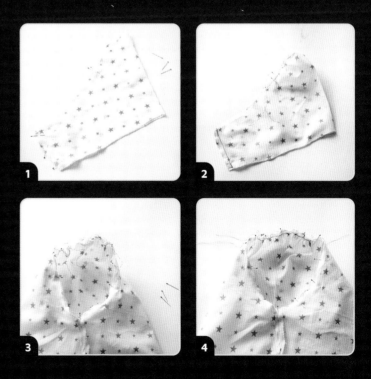

SEWING RAGLAN SLEEVES

Raglan sleeves do not have a shoulder seam because the top of the sleeve forms the shoulder. This is the easiest sleeve to get right.

1. Mark the front and back of the sleeves; the markings are given on the pattern. It is customary to mark the back with two lines or two pins, and the front with one line or pin.

2. Lay the garment flat, front side up. Place the sleeve on top, back side up. This way, the sleeve and armhole are right sides together. Match the front of the sleeve with the front of the armhole. Stitch.

3. Place the back of the sleeve over the back armhole, right sides together. Stitch. The top of the sleeve is now part of the neckline.

4. To close the garment, stitch the side in one seam from the cuff to the bottom of the garment.

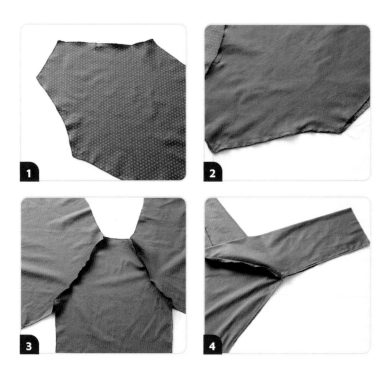

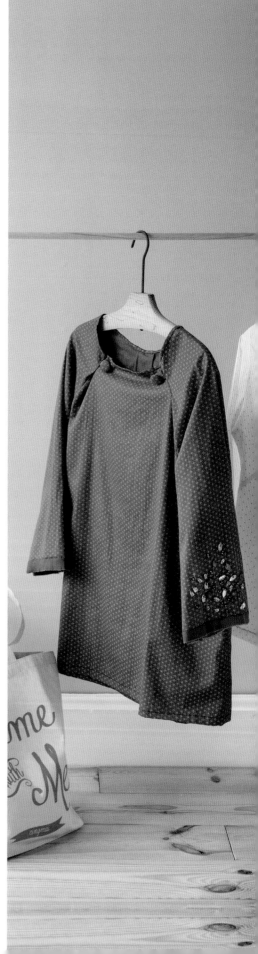

CREATING PUFFED SLEEVES

If you can make gathers on the sleeves, you can also make pleats and give them volume. This is especially true for puffed sleeves.

1. These sleeves are made with two layers of fabric to add structure and volume. Cut four sleeve pieces. For each sleeve pin two sleeves right sides together and stitch around all outside edges to join.

2. Open the sewn sleeve and lay it flat. Form the two large flat pleats on the bottom of the sleeve, referring to the marks given on the pattern. Pin the pleats to hold them in place. The bottom of the sleeve will be the same length as the sleeve hem facing.

3. Place the facing over the sleeve, over the bottom of the sleeve right sides together. Machine stitch.

4. Stitch two gathering threads at the top of the sleeves between the marks given on the pattern. Gather the sleeves slightly. Pin the sleeve, right sides together, to the armhole. Pin the ungathered part evenly to the bottom of the armhole and pull on the gathering threads at the top to distribute evenly. The sleeve should be the same diameter as the armhole. Pin. Stitch the sleeve into the armhole. Fold the facing to the inside of the sleeve so it covers the stitching line and press. Complete the garment by sewing the sleeve and side seams and then sewing the facing in place inside the bottom of the sleeve.

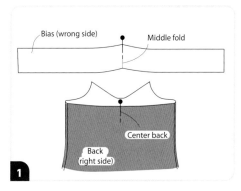

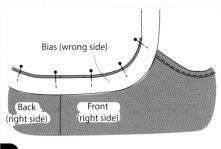

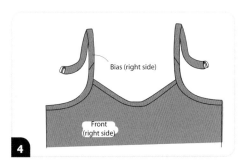

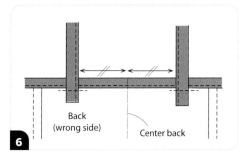

Bias can be used for making straps for a top.

1. Cut a bias strip according to the pattern measurements. Fold the strip widthwise to mark its middle, and stick a pin in vertically. Do the same with the center back of the tank top.

2. Lay the bias strip on the upper back of the tank top, right sides together and edge to edge. Continue pinning to the top of the armhole on the front band.

3. Stitch with a sewing machine (elastic stitch or small zigzag and jersey needle) like you would bias tape, but stop at the border formed by the front band.

Fold over the rest of the strip so that it is the same width as the bias tape already sewn onto the tank top. Remember to join the ends on the inside of the strips. Pin the two remaining strips together along the entire length.

4. Stitch with a sewing machine (elastic stitch or small zigzag and jersey needle) for adjustable straps. For less elasticity, do the same thing but change to a straight stitch.

5. Position the straps on the back of the tank top, making sure they are pinned well inside the back and evenly spaced from the sides.

6. Stitch the bottom of the straps to the back of the tank top.

7. Press.

POCKETS

SEWING A PATCH POCKET

There are very few garments without pockets, and if you happen to have any, you have surely missed pockets from time to time! The patch pocket is the easiest to make.

BY HAND

1. Carefully cut the fabric into the desired shape. Fold in the raw edges evenly towards the wrong side. Press to mark the fold.

2. Place the pocket where you want it. Pin evenly, with the pin points facing inward, so you don't prick yourself while sewing.

3. Begin sewing, leaving a long tail of thread so you can tie a knot and hide it on the back side.

4. Stitch on three sides to leave the top opening.

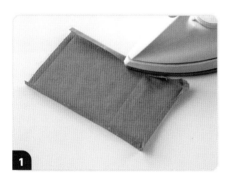

BY MACHINE

The technique is the same as for hand sewing.

1. Cut out a pocket. Fold in ⅝″ (1.5cm) on the top side of the pocket. Press. Stitch forming the top pocket hem.

2. Fold in ⅜″ (1cm) on the other three sides. Press to hold in place.

3. Clip the corners.

4. Place the pocket on the front of the main fabric. Pin and stitch on all three sides ³⁄₁₆″ (0.5cm) from the edge to leave the top opening.

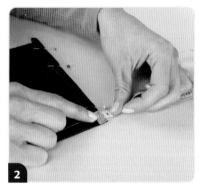

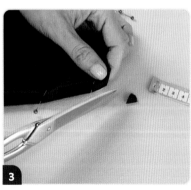

SEWING A ROUND PATCH POCKET

The patch pocket can be made in a rounded version. To make it, you can borrow the template technique from patchwork.

1. Cut a pocket template from lightweight cardboard. The template should be ⅜″ (1cm) smaller than the fabric ³⁄₁₆″ × 2 (0.5cm). Pin the template to the fabric. Fold down the top if you want a pocket with a flat opening. Hem this top edge by folding under and stitching.

2. Machine stitch flush with the cardboard template using large stitches.

3. Pull slightly on the sewing thread. The fabric will fold over the cardboard. Press to keep the shape. Remove the cardboard.

4. Pin the fabric circle to the garment. Sew the pocket by hand or machine.

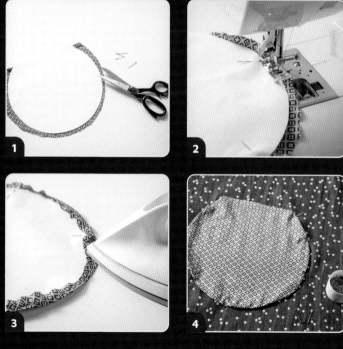

You can add a flap to the pocket. The flap is always lined and attached to the garment or project above the pocket.

1. Position the pocket using your markings. Pin it in place. If you have lined the pocket, place the opening used to turn it at the bottom of the pocket.

2. Topstitch both sides and the bottom of the pocket. To reinforce your stitching, at the top of the pocket on each side stitch two tiny triangles with the sewing machine: one at the beginning of the seam and one at the end. To do this, stitch to the pocket opening along the edge of the fold, then lift the presser foot to turn. Lower it down and make a few stitches along the pocket opening. At the corner, insert the needle back into the work, raise the presser foot, and turn and lower it. Then continue your topstitching until you reach the last corner and repeat the process from the beginning, but in reverse!

3. Cut the two flap pieces from the fabric and one from interfacing. Cut ³⁄₁₆″ (0.5cm) around the interfacing flap piece and place it textured side down on one of the two pocket flaps. Press for a few seconds to fuse. The iron must be very hot, and you must not use steam.

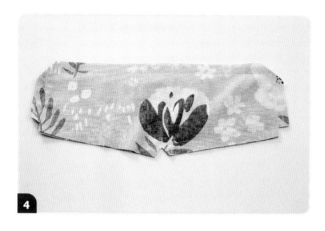

4. When your piece has cooled, place the two flaps right sides together and pin. Sew all around, leaving a small opening for turning at the top of the flap. Trim the corners and point of the flap.

5. Turn right side out through the opening and press the piece well, rolling the seams to the wrong side. Topstitch around the flap, except for the top.

Position the flap over the pocket using your markings. Pin and topstitch to the garment along the top edge of the flap. Make your buttonhole on the flap (after testing on a scrap of interfacing). Open it with the seam ripper. Stitch your button on the front of the pocket.

SEWING AN ELASTIC POCKET

The elastic pocket is a rectangle held together by a band of elastic. It is a practical solution to sew on the inside of a tote bag and is very easy to make.

1. On one of the long sides of the pocket rectangle, make a hem by pressing the fabric twice ⅜″ (1cm) to the back side. Pin this hem to hold it in place.

2. Stitch ⅛″ (3mm) from the edge of the inside fold. You've created the casing for your elastic.

3. Attach a safety pin onto your piece of elastic. Slide your safety pin and elastic through the casing and out the other end.

4. Stitch the elastic 3/16″ (0.5cm) from the edges (more secure than a pin). Distribute the gathers across the width of the pocket.

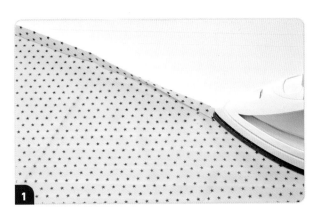

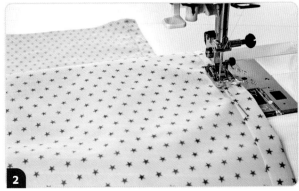

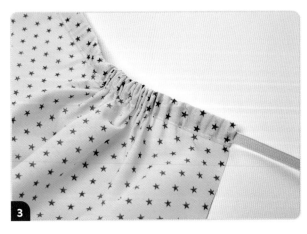

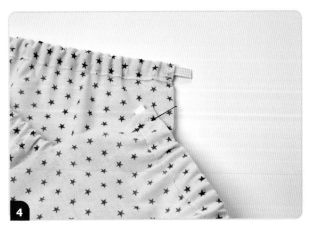

5. On the opposite side, sew gathering stitches and gather the bottom of the pocket. Place it front side up on top of the main fabric. Pin and stitch around the edge of the pocket ³⁄₁₆″ (0.5cm) from the edges.

6. Remove the gathering threads.

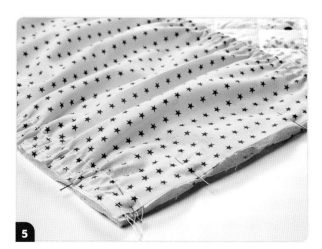

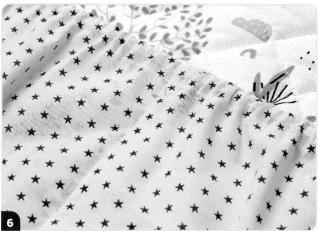

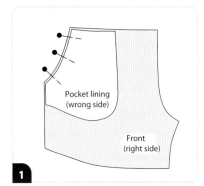

Pocket lining
(wrong side)

Front
(right side)

1

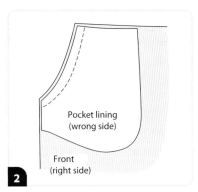

Pocket lining
(wrong side)

Front
(right side)

2

SEWING A SLANT POCKET

The slant pocket is sewn at an angle from the waistband to the side seam of the garment. It is found in both pants and skirts.

1. Take the top of pocket lining and place it on the front of the garment at the pocket opening, right sides of the fabric together. Position the curve of the pocket lining along the curve of the pocket opening in the garment. Pin in place.

2. Stitch ³⁄₁₆″ (0.5cm) from the edge.

3. Turn the pocket lining inside out and topstitch ³⁄₁₆″ (0.5cm) from the edge.

4. Pin the pocket lining and the second pocket piece, the larger one that will be next to the body, right sides together, forming the pocket bag.

5. Stitch ³⁄₁₆″ (0.5cm) from the edge all around the pocket (leaving the top of the pocket bag unstitched).

6. Finally, pin the top of the pocket to the front of the garment.

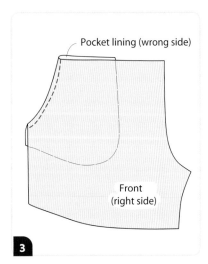

Pocket lining (wrong side)

Front
(right side)

3

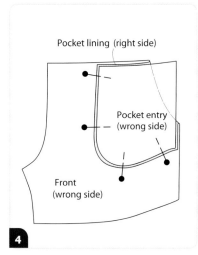

Pocket lining (right side)

Pocket entry
(wrong side)

Front
(wrong side)

4

The zippered pocket is often sewn inside a bag and sometimes also is used in sportswear. It requires a little skill.

1. Trace the pocket window on the piece cut from the lining, the same length as the intended zipper. Stitch.

2. Cut and notch, then press the seam allowance to the back side to create the pocket window.

3. Position the zipper by placing the zipper faceup under the window and topstitching around the window.

4. Line the pocket with a pocket lining of the same shape.

5. Sew the lining with the zipper opening and the rest of the bag lining before assembling the bag lining with the bag, or continue with garment construction.

1

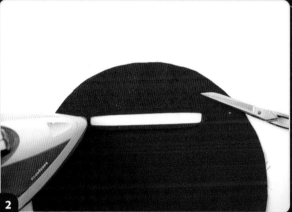
2

3

4

WAISTBANDS

SEWING AN ELASTIC WAISTBAND IN A SKIRT

This simple way to make a skirt is also a great first project.

1. Fold the top of the fabric over 1⅛″ (3cm). Use pins to hold the fabric in place. Stitch along the bottom of the fold to create a casing. Leave about 2″ (5cm) unstitched.

2. Attach a large safety pin to an elastic band and feed it through the casing. The elastic's width should be less than the width of the casing.

3. Adjust the length of the elastic to your waist size. Sew the two ends of the elastic flat by overlapping them.

4. Close the unstitched opening with small slip stitches.

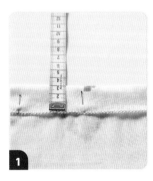

SEWING A STRETCH WAISTBAND ONTO A SKIRT

This waistband is made in a jersey fabric, which gives it its elasticity. You can stitch it with a serger or the zigzag stitch on the sewing machine.

1. Create gathering stitches on the top of the skirt (front and back) if the skirt's waistline is much larger than the waistband.

2. Close the waistband by pinning the short sides together, right sides together, and stitching ³⁄₁₆″ (0.5cm) from the edge. You now have a ring. Fold the waistband ring in half, wrong sides together.

3. Pin the closed waistband to the top of the skirt, right sides together: To position the waistband, place the seam of the waistband so it is facing the right side seam. Then fold the band in half and pin all around the rest of the waistband.

4. Sew the waistband to the top of the skirt ³⁄₁₆″ (0.5cm) from the edges.

5. Press.

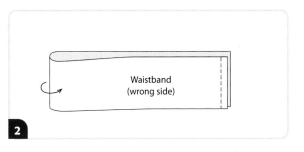

Waistband
(wrong side)

2

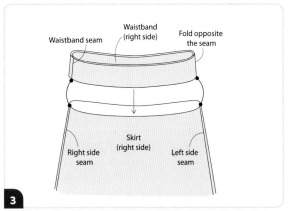

Waistband seam
Waistband (right side)
Fold opposite the seam
Right side seam
Skirt (right side)
Left side seam

3

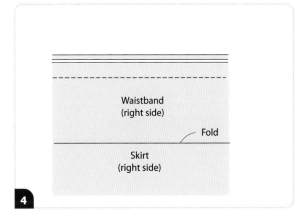

Waistband
(right side)
Fold
Skirt
(right side)

4

SEWING A WAISTBAND THAT INCLUDES A ZIPPER

In this treatment the zipper goes right to the top of the attached waistband.

1. Pin the ends of the large front waistband to the two back waistband pieces. Stitch the together at the sides seams with a ³⁄₁₆″ (0.5cm) seam allowance with a serger or the zigzag stitch on the sewing machine.

2. Fold the resulting strip lengthwise, wrong sides together, and press.

3. Open the waistband piece and pin one edge to the top of the skirt, right side together, positioning the waistband seams at the side seams of the skirt.

4. Sew the waistband and skirt top ³⁄₁₆″ (0.5cm) from the edges with a serger or sewing machine.

5. Sew the zipper to the back of the skirt and right up through the waistband making sure the zipper ends just before the pressed fold in the center of the waistband piece.

6. Fold the remaining half of the waistband down over the top of the zipper. Press the waistband. Press the seam allowances to the bottom of the skirt to reduce bulk and sew the waistband down along the waistline by topstitching close to the seam line from the right side.

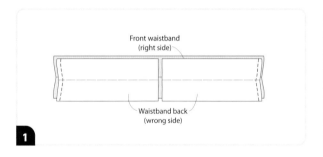

Front waistband (right side)

Waistband back (wrong side)

1

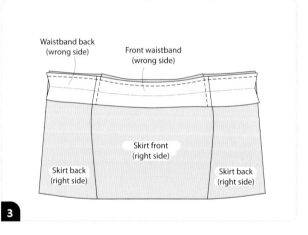

Waistband back (wrong side)

Front waistband (wrong side)

Skirt front (right side)

Skirt back (right side)

Skirt back (right side)

3

SEWING A FACED WAISTBAND

The waistband facing is a piece added to the inside of the skirt to give it a little structure and eliminates the need for a sewn-on waistband. The facing piece has the same shape as the top of the skirt.

1. Position the waistband facing pieces front sides together. Pin the short sides. Stitch and press open the seams.

2. Position the facing on the top of the skirt, right sides together. Match the waistband seams with the skirt seams. Sew ³⁄₁₆″ (0.5cm) from the edge or the seam allowance specified on the pattern.

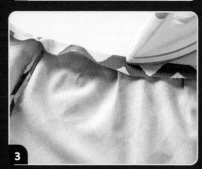

3. Turn the facing over to the wrong side of the skirt. Press and make a small slip stitch to tack the facing just at the seams.

4. Stitch the top of the skirt ⅛″ (0.3cm) from the edge.

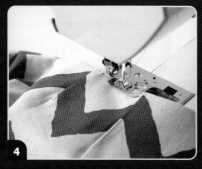

Giving a Back Shape and Form
BY ADDING A YOKE PIECE

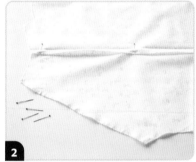

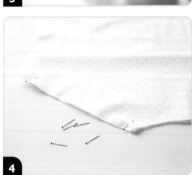

SEWING A YOKE

Sewing a yoke will give a shirt more shape, especially if the fabric is thin.

1. After cutting the yoke according to the pattern, press under the bottom edge to the wrong side about ⅜″ (1cm) (measurements are given on the pattern or in the explanation).

2. Lay the back garment piece flat, wrong side up. Place the yoke on the top, right side up. Match the edges, then carefully fold the yoke down towards the hem edge so you can see the pressing line of the hem fold.

3. Stitch the bottom of the yoke to the back along this fold line.

4. Fold the yoke back up on top of the back. Press. Pin and baste at the shoulders to attach the yoke to the top of the back. Assemble the garment as usual.

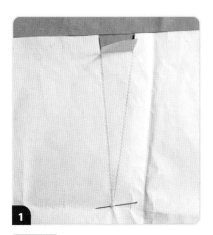
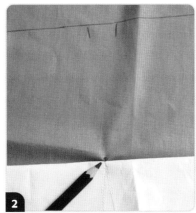
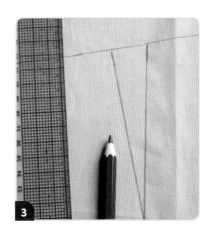

DARTS

A classic in sewing, darts allow a garment to be fitted to the body. Darts are marked on the pattern with a long triangle.

TRANSFERRING A DART TO THE FABRIC

1. To correctly transfer a dart, mark the two points forming the triangle's base with a chalk pencil.

2. Place a pin at the tip of your dart, and fold the pattern up to that pin.

3. Mark this point with a chalk pencil; then, once the pattern is completely removed, join the three points.

4. To transfer the dart to the other side (if you are working on the fabric folded in half), with the pattern facing you, place pins—making sure to take both layers of fabric—on the three ends of the triangle forming the dart, turn your piece over, and make a chalk mark at the three points marked by the pins. Join these three points: Your dart is drawn.

TIP

You can also mark the darts using tailor's tacks (or loop stitches). To make a tailor's tack, using a thread color that contrasts with your fabric, thread a needle, so you are left with two long threads of equal length. Then at every point to be marked, make a stitch through all layers of fabric, leaving a long thread tail.

Make a second stitch over the first, inserting the needle where the thread exits. Instead of pulling the thread, leave a loop on the surface. Cut it off, leaving a long thread tail.

Cut the loop in half and gently lift the paper pattern free.

Carefully separate the layers of fabric, leaving a length of thread between each; then cut the threads between them. The markings are now on the fabric. Remember to remove the tailor's tacks before stitching a seam; otherwise, they might be caught in the stitching and difficult to remove. If there are still a few threads left in the fabric, use tweezers to remove them.

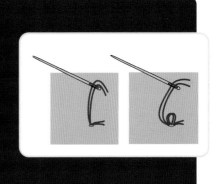

MAKING DARTS

To accurately shape the dart before sewing it, it is best to first baste it closed by hand.

1. After drawing the dart lines on the front side of the fabric with chalk or another removable marking pen, stitch at the base of the triangle from underneath on one of the lines (A).

2. Go straight to the other side (B). Move down the dart and then back a little bit below point A. Continue until you reach the tip of the dart.

3. On the top, you have a series of lines parallel to line AB. When the thread is pulled tight, the stitches disappear from the right side and the dart fabric is on the back. Finish by machine stitching the dart on the marked line.

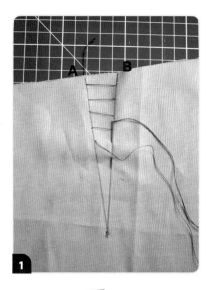
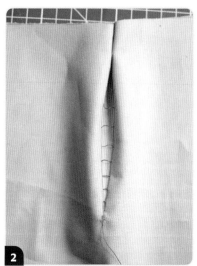
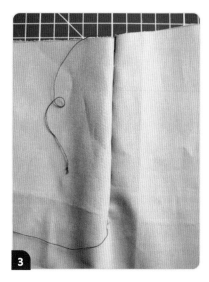

ATTENTION

To get a neat end, stick a pin in the point between the two layers of fabric before pressing.

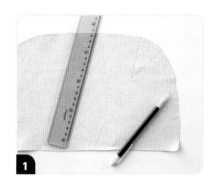

SEWING DARTS BY HAND

Darts are used to create or absorb volume and sculpt fabric. They are more often used on garments, but they also have their place on accessories.

1. Transfer the dart design (location and size) accurately to the back side of the fabric.

2. Fold the fabric right sides together, overlapping the two long sides of the triangle, so that the stitching is on the wrong side of the garment.

3. Stitch along the line. The top of the triangle should be very thin and almost parallel to the fabric.

4. Press the dart by folding it over to one side. Note that you do not cut the inside of a dart.

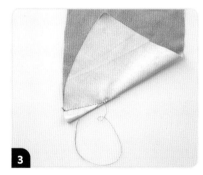

THE BUST DART

Bust darts are a key detail where a garment can be adjusted for a precise, personalized fit.

1. Transfer the marks given on the pattern to the fabric. You can draw the darts with a water-soluble fabric marker. It's convenient, and the line will fade quickly with a bit of water. Mark the darts on both pattern pieces.

2. Fold the fabric, right sides together, lining up the two long lengths of the dart triangle.

3. Machine stitch the dart. Start at the wide end of the triangle and work your way to the tip. The dart is sewn onto the wrong side of the fabric.

4. Press the dart by folding it down. Do not cut the dart.
Repeat on the other side for the second dart.

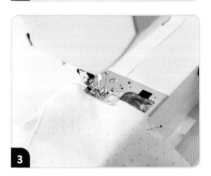

BACK DARTS

Back darts are also used to fine-tune the fit of a garment and look like long, narrow diamonds. They are stitched in two steps.

1. Transfer the dart markings from the pattern to both pattern pieces. Place pins or draw the darts with a fabric marker.

2. Right sides together fold the fabric along the length of the dart, from one marked end to the other.

3. Start stitching the dart from the middle of the dart, the widest part. Carefully stitch to one end of the dart.

4. Stitch the second part of the dart diamond, starting at the middle. Starting in the middle allows you to stitch narrower darts more easily. Press the darts toward the center of the garment.

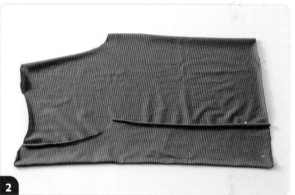

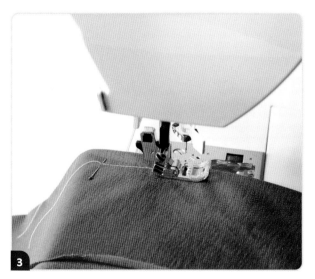

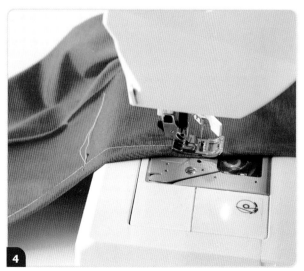

LARGE FRONT DARTS (SIDE DARTS)

Large front darts are useful when fitting a dress to the body, as more fabric is needed at the bust and hip area and less at the waist.

1. Mark the darts on both pattern pieces. You can mark with pins or draw the darts with chalk or fabric marker on the fabric.

2. Fold the fabric, right sides together, so that the marked dart legs line up.

3. Machine stitch the dart.

4. Press by folding the dart towards the middle of the piece.

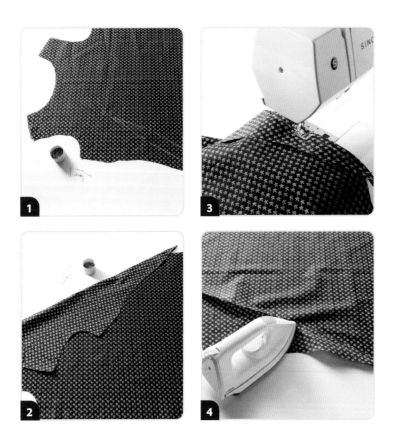

FANCY PLEATS

Making small fancy pleats brings a little fullness to a garment. Dressing them up with a fancy stitch also helps to disguise the stitching lines.

1. Transfer the pleat markings from the pattern to the front side of the fabric.

2. On each mark, make a small fold ⅛″ (0.3cm) deep. Fold the fabric over the mark. Secure with a pin. Baste.

3. Stitch on each fold with a pretty decorative stitch. Remove the basting thread.

4. Pull the threads to the back side. Make a discreet knot by tying the main thread with the bobbin thread.

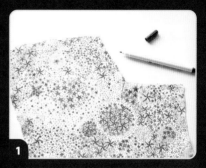

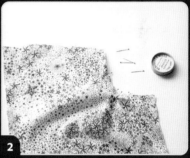

BOX PLEATS

Box pleats are two folds laid side by side, with the fold lines facing each other and so the excess fabric is on the inside. Often sewn into skirts, they add a pretty, fancy touch. When purchasing fabric, be aware that pleats require much more fabric.

1. Transfer all the pleat marks given on the pattern to the fabric. Pin the pleats in place as marked.

2. Make a first half of the pleat. Crease along the marked fold line and then lay this fold so it is even with the marked pleat center line.

3. Make the second half of the pleat in the same way, this time folding so this fold line meets the first pleat in the middle at the marked pleat center line.

4. Secure the pleats in position to the waistline with either discrete machine stitching or hand basting. This stitching will allow you to continue work without pins.

TIP

To prevent the box pleat from opening when the garment is finished, slightly overlap the two pleat edges instead of placing them side by side.

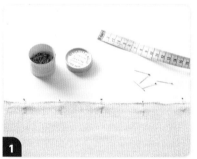

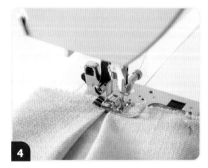

OTHER PLEATS

There are many different kinds of pleats to embellish your work. Here are a few of them.

ROUND PLEATS (A)

These are two flat folds in opposite directions, one to the right and one to the left. If you make several round pleats next to each other, you will have a round pleat, a box pleat, a round pleat, and so on.

Mark the folds with an iron. Fold. Iron again to hold in place. Pin in place.

RIBBED PLEATS (B)

This is a very fine pleat. It was once used in lingerie. Each pleat is about ⅛″ (2 or 3mm). Each pleat is sewn at ¹⁄₁₆″ (1mm), and you can run them vertically or horizontally. Make this pleat in thin fabrics.

FLAT PLEATS (C)

These are overlapping pleats. This is the principle of pleated skirts! It is essential to have a clean-cut rectangle in the fabric to draw them correctly. Pleats use between two and three times more material than routine work.

1. To draw even flat pleats, use a ruler and tailor's chalk. Place regular markings. If necessary, number the pleats.

2. Fold evenly. Press to hold the pleats in place.

3. Stitch each fold ¹⁄₁₆″ to ⅛″ (1 to 2mm) from the edge for several inches.

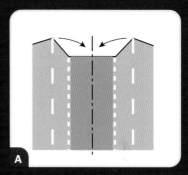

A

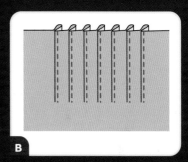

B

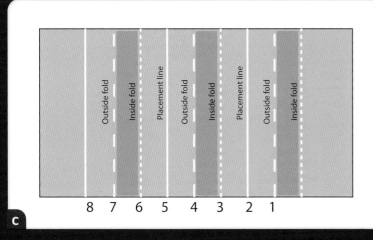

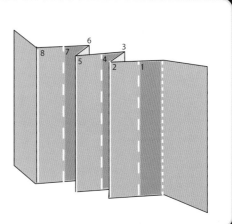

C

THE ORGAN PIPE PLEATS

Organ pipe pleats (sometimes called organ pleats or projected pleats) are a series of small vertical folds held together across the pleats. They are created with a solid thread, or cord, and stitched by hand. The cording runs through the middle of the pleats (the fabric will fold loosely in and out on either side of the cord). This process allows for the absorption or distribution of a large width of fabric, in this case a bag.

1. Mark the locations of the folds with chalk or an erasable pen and then mark a line midway between the folds.

2. Take a thick piece of thread or fine cord and tie a big knot. Run the thread evenly along the length 1⅛″ (3cm) from the edge on each end, then in and out on every other line.

3. Repeat twice more, making sure to be moving in and out of the fabric in the same places.

4. After assembling the body of the bag, pull the threads together to bring the pleats into a fan shape and tie a secure knot.

PLEATS ON CURTAINS (WITH SHIRRING OR PLEATING TAPE)

Shirirng or pleating tape is sewn onto the back of curtains to gather or pleat them and hang them. It is easy to sew, although recently large eyelets often replace it.

1. Fold the fabric 1⅛″ (3cm) inward. Press. Secure the fold with pins.

2. Pin the pleating tape evenly to the folded edge, ⅝″ (1.5cm) from the top. Remove the pins from the fold line.

3. Fold in each end ⅜″ (1cm) of the fabric and the pleating tape to finish neatly.

4. Stitch the taped ³⁄₁₆″ (0.5cm) from the edge. Do not stitch the cord ends (you will pull the cords if needed to make a gathered curtain).

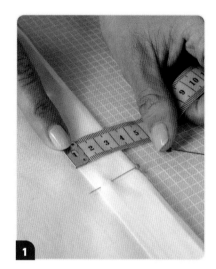

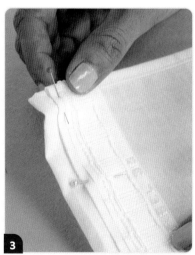

BLINDS

To create a set of slides to raise and lower blinds, you must hand sew rings in a line for this purpose, through which the cording will pass. Let's assume that the blind is about 55″ (140cm) high (and has 24 rings).

1. On the wrong side of the fabric, mark a point in the center of the material and 4″ (10cm) from the edge.

2. Mark a second point 6″ (15cm) above the first.

3. Mark seven points in a line 6″ (15cm) apart.

4. Sew the rings with a single stitch, but repeat several times so the ring is free to move but secure.

5. Cut three lengths of 73″ (185cm), 90″ (230cm), and 112″ (285cm) of curtain cord. Tie the 112″ (285cm) cord in the first ring on the left, slip it through the seven rings above, and then thread it through the three pulleys.

Tie the 90″ (230cm) cord in the middle ring, slip it through the seven rings above, then through the central and double pulley. Knot the 73″ (185cm) cord in the right ring, and slip it through the seven rings above and then through the double pulley.

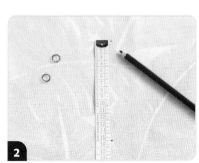

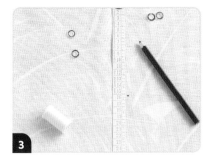

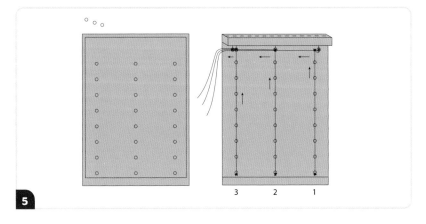

GATHERS

Gathering will give fullness and movement to some garments. It is also the basis of sleeve construction.

1. Run two gathering threads across the top of the fabric, ⅛" (3mm) apart. The gathering stitch is a large straight stitch. You can sew it by hand or by machine by setting the machine stitch length to a very long stitch. Always run two lines of stitching parallel to each other for better distribution of the gathers. There is no need to tie knots at the ends of the threads, as they are removed afterward.

2. Pull the gathering threads on both sides of the fabric gently to adjust the fabric to the desired length. Work with the bobbin threads; they are easier to pull.

3. Continue with construction, placing the machine stitches between the two gathering threads.

4. Remove the gathering threads by gently pulling them out.

TIP

The smaller the stitches, the closer the gathers.

When basting a gathered piece to another, occasionally backstitch to prevent the gathers from slipping.

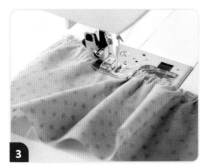

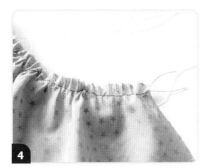

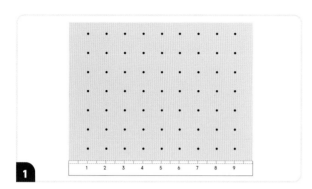

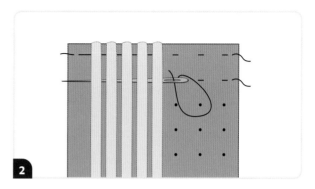

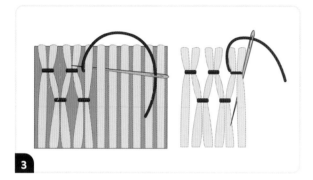

SMOCKING

These small pleats originated in the work smocks worn in the countries of Central Europe in the Middle Ages. Use soft fabrics for nice gathers and a special elastic thread for smocking.

1. To make the smocking, draw a precise grid on the area you want smocked with a water-soluble fabric marker. Allow a minimum of ¼″ (7mm) between marks for thin fabrics and ½″ to ⅝″ (12 to 14mm) for thick fabrics.

2. To baste the gathers, create a gathering stitch by hand, passing a thread through each intersection point in one row. Use a colored thread that contrasts with the fabric to make it easier to follow when embroidering. Repeat with each row.

3. Pull the threads to gather the fabric, preferably pulling each thread at the same time. The gathering is done like regular gathers. Stop the threads when the entire surface of the gathers is even. Now add embroidery stitches to connect gathers to form the smocking, offsetting the connected gathers in each row. Embroider zigzags or polka dots ... whatever you like!

4. Remove the gathering threads.

TIP

Use a large width of fabric. The width should be about four times the width of the finished smocking.

HEMMING *and* FINISHING

THESE ARE USUALLY THE FINAL TOUCHES. HEMS ARE GENERALLY INVISIBLE; THEY ARE, THEREFORE, TRADITIONALLY DONE BY HAND. PRESS UP THE HEM ALLOWANCES FIRST BEFORE STITCHING.

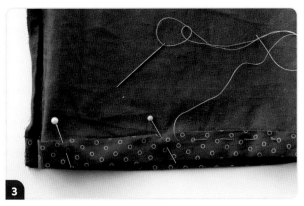

THE FLAT HEM BY HAND

The flat hem is easy and quick to sew. Don't forget to iron the folds, though!

1. Fold ⅜″ (1cm) to the wrong side of the fabric. Press. Fold down ¾″ (2cm). Press to hold folds in place.

2. Pin evenly, with the pin points facing down to avoid pricking yourself.

3. Baste by sewing with large straight stitches to hold the hem in place. Remove pins as you go.

4. Stitch with a slip stitch. Tuck as much thread as possible into the hem.

THE FLAT HEM BY MACHINE

Machine hemming has the advantage of being fast. It allows you to finish decorative items but also jeans quickly.

1. On one short side, fold ³⁄₁₆″ (0.5cm) to the inside. Press.

2. Fold over ⁵⁄₈″ (1.5cm) again. Press. Secure with pins.

3. Stitch along the edge of the fold in one seam.

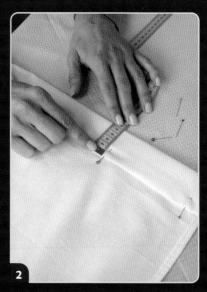

THE ROLLED HEM

The rolled hem is very useful for thin fabrics. First, iron the fabric beforehand. The fabric must be cut clean and straight.

1. Fold ⅛″ (0.3cm) to the wrong side of the fabric. Press to hold the fold in place.

2. Fold over again ³⁄₁₆″ (0.4cm). Press. Stitch the hem with a slip stitch.

HEM CORNERS

This pretty beveled corner finish is used a lot in decorating, quilts, tablecloths, napkins, and more. This double-sided treatment requires care and preparation.

1. Draw a margin at ⅜″ (1cm) from the edge, then a line at 2⅜″ (6cm). Determine the middle and draw a triangle. Proceed in the same way on all the ends.

2. Place a second strip, front sides together, under the first strip, and sew the tip of the triangle.

3. Cut off ⅜″ (1cm) from the tip. Sew the other two strips together to form the frame.

4. Turn the frame right side out and poke out the corners. Press for a perfect finish.

5. Pin both sides of the main piece to the frame. Stitch, leaving an opening, if necessary (to insert a cushion or stuffing). Close the opening.

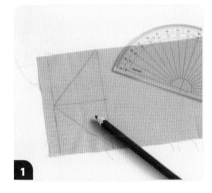

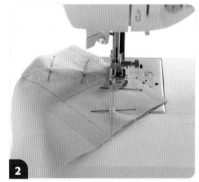

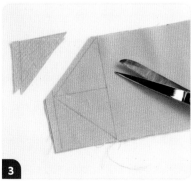

ELASTIC CUFFS

Putting elastic at the bottom of the sleeves is the easiest solution for beginners.

1. At the bottom of the sleeves, make the casing. To do this press a ⅜″ (1cm) and then a ¾″ (2cm) hem.

2. Topstitch ⅛″ (2mm) along the folded edge of the hem.

3. Make sure to leave a small opening in this line of stitching to slip your elastic in.

4. Slip elastic into the hems with a safety pin.

5. Secure the ends of the elastic with a few stitches.

6. Close the opening.

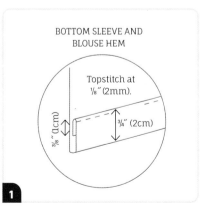

BOTTOM SLEEVE AND BLOUSE HEM

Topstitch at ⅛″ (2mm).

⅜″ (1cm)

¾″ (2cm)

1

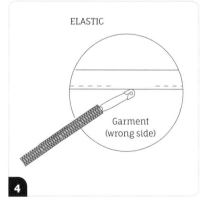

ELASTIC

Garment (wrong side)

4

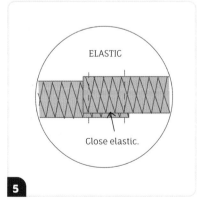

ELASTIC

Close elastic.

5

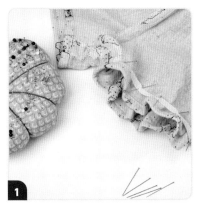

**The elastic finish of a bloomer is
a great way to learn the technique
of sewing elastic directly into a
garment.**

1. Depending on the size made, cut the
recommended amount of elastic for
the thigh circumference. The marking
process may seem awkward but will
quickly make sense. Make a mark with
a pencil halfway down your elastic.

Do the same to find the middle of the
thigh circumference on the bloomer
leg. Locate your notch at the crotch
seam—pin one end of your elastic there.
Then pin the middle of the elastic to
the middle of the thigh. Place the other
end of the elastic next to where you
started. You will then pull to distribute
the amount of fabric on the elastic by
pinning at regular intervals.

2. Remove the table from your sewing
machine to free the arm. Then select
the elastic stitch. To sew evenly, line
up the center of the elastic with the
center of your presser foot. Insert your
needle. Go slowly, pulling on the fabric
and elastic.

3. Repeat for the other leg.

BLOUSE CUFFS

There are many ways to finish sleeve edges. The simple cuff is the easiest.

1. Create a slit at the bottom of the sleeve. The slits at the bottom of the sleeves are usually 2¾″ (7cm) high.

2. Press a ⅜″ (1cm) seam allowance on each side of the bias, wrong sides together.

3. Fold the bias in half lengthwise and press.

4. Position your bias along the slit.

5. Topstitch the bias to the sleeve slits at ⅛″ (2mm).

6. On the back side of the sleeve, place the two bias layers on top of each other and stitch a 45° angle at the top of the slit.

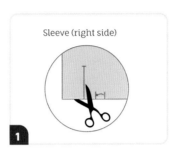

Sleeve (right side)

1

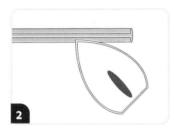

2

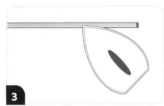

3

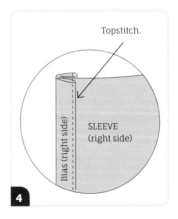

Topstitch.

Bias (right side)

SLEEVE (right side)

4

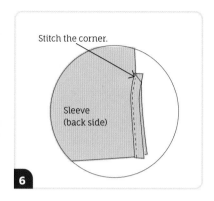

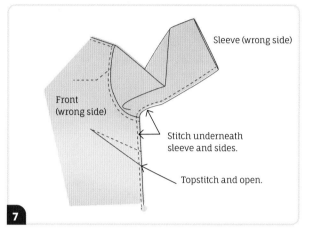

7. Pin the sleeves to the body, front sides together. Stitch armhole, then the underside of the sleeve.

8. Press ⅜″ (1cm) fold under on the bottom of the cuff.

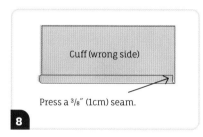

9. Fold the cuff with the right sides together (the side without the fold is ⅜″ (1cm) higher than the side with the fold).

10. Stitch the ends.

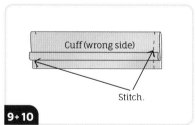

11. Stitch the side that does not have the folded edge on the wrong side of the sleeve, right sides together.

12. Fold side with folded edge to the right side of the sleeve and topstitch ⅛″ (2mm).

13. Make the buttonholes.

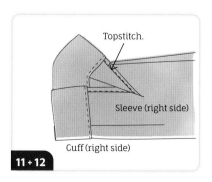

MAKING AND APPLYING RIBBING

To finish a sweater or a pair of pants, you can sew some ribbing at the end of sleeves, the bottom of a sweater, or the bottom of pants. You have two possibilities: Buy them ready-made in the round, or cut and sew them yourself from ribbing sold by the yard.

1. Generally, the end of the garment on which the ribbing will be sewn has a slightly larger diameter than the ribbing. If it is much larger, stitch gathering threads to the edge of the garment ends.

To make your own ribbing, trace the required strip(s) on the back side of your ribbing sold by the yard with a tape measure, then cut out.

If you have already purchased a sewn ribbing, see Step 5.

2. Close the strip(s) by pinning the short sides front sides together and stitching ³⁄₁₆˝ (0.5cm) from the edge. This creates a ring.

3. Fold the strip(s) wrong sides together.

4. Pin the strip(s) edge to edge and right sides together on the end of the garment (sleeve, leg, and so on). It is easiest to place the band around the sleeve or leg. Position the seam of the band so it is facing the stitching on the underside of the sleeve or the inside of the leg.

5. Sew the band ³⁄₁₆˝ (0.5cm) from the edges.

6. Press.

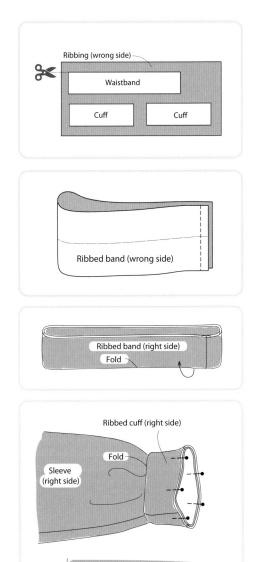

CLOSURES *and* FASTENERS

BUTTONS

COVERING A BUTTON

Using buttons covered in the same fabric as the garment or in a contrasting fabric adds a refined touch to a project. Ready-to-cover button assembly kits include button components and crimping accessories.

1. Cut a scrap piece of fabric into a circle. The circle's diameter should be slightly larger ⅛″–³⁄₁₆″ (3–4mm) than the diameter of the button. Manufacturers offer cutting templates in their kits.

2. Run a gathering thread around the fabric circle.

3. Place the part to be covered on the round piece's back side. Gently pull the thread to gather the piece and cover the fabric button. Tie off the thread.

4. Clip the shank piece onto the covered button. The stitching is hidden.

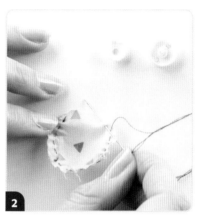

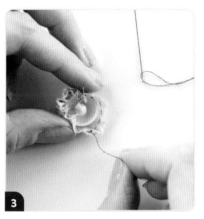

TIP

If you don't have a button to cover, you can use any scrap button using this method. Just be sure to sew the underside of the button well so that it's clean.

When covering a button, it is important to use very thin fabrics to hide the excess behind the part of the form with the shank.

SEWING A FLAT BUTTON

To allow for flexibility when buttoning, the flat button should not be sewn too close to the fabric.

1. Insert a match between the fabric and the button. Pull the thread out through one of the holes in the button. Put it through another hole. Repeat several times.

2. Remove the match. Wrap the sewing threads between the button and the garment to create a button shank.

3. Have fun styling by sewing in an anchor, square, cross, or parallel pattern.

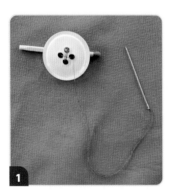

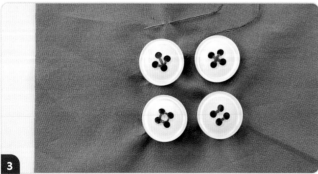

SEWING A BUTTON WITH A SHANK

Some buttons have shankst, so you must pass the needle through the shankt and fabric several times.

The shank of the button is already acting as a riser.

Pull the thread out from underneath to hide the knot under the fabric. Pass the thread and needle through the hole in the shank and back into the material. Repeat several times.

Tie a knot. Cut the thread.

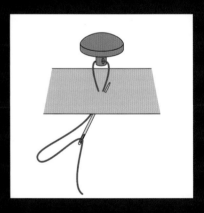

TIP

Sometimes seams and threads are stronger than textiles. If it gets caught somewhere, the button will not fall off but tear the garment. If your fabric is very thin, don't hesitate to cut a small piece of fabric and sew it behind the button for reinforcement.

BUTTONHOLES

EMBROIDERING BUTTONHOLES BY HAND

This technique is similar to embroidery. To succeed, it is necessary to get used to the rhythm of the buttonhole stitches.

1. Mark the location and length of the buttonhole with a water-soluble fabric marker or chalk.

2. Slit the buttonhole cleanly.

3. Embroider a couple of large straight stitches perpendicular to the buttonhole at each end.

4. Stitch on the back side, and exit on the front side of the slit. Make a loop with the thread; then pull the thread through the loop. Pull the thread gently to form the buttonhole stitch.

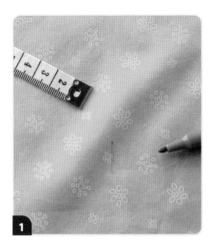

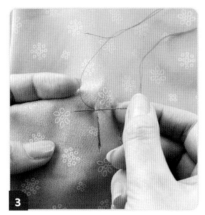

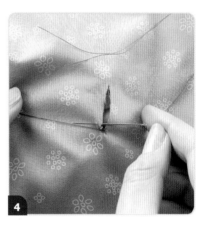

TIP

To determine the width of the buttonhole, cut a strip of paper. Wrap the paper around the button through its middle. Mark where the paper overlaps, then cut the strip. Fold the strip in half down the middle. This will give you the length of the buttonhole.

Start with the least visible buttonholes (for practice) and end with the buttonholes near the collar, those which are most visible.

MAKING BUTTONHOLES USING THE MACHINE

Buttonholes can be sewn easily on the machine by using the right accessories.

1. Draw the location of the buttonhole with tailor's chalk or a fabric marker.

2. Determine the diameter of the button using a sewing gauge with a sliding marker for the buttonhole size. It will be slightly ⅛″ (3mm) larger than the diameter of the button.

3. Remove the presser foot from the machine.

4. Fit the special buttonhole presser foot provided in the machine's accessory box.

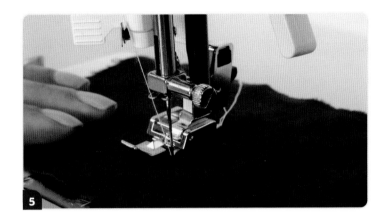

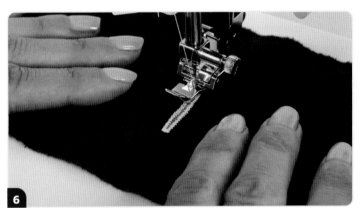

5. Stitch the first side of the buttonhole using the machine's buttonhole program or tight zigzag stitch.

6. Stitch a machine bar tack at one end of the buttonhole. Your machine may have a setting for this, or you can do it yourself by widening the zigzag stitch width and shortening the stitch length. To stitch the second side: Some machines have a function to do this directly. If this is not the case, stitch the second side in a very tight zigzag stitch in reverse. Stitch a second machine bar tack to close the buttonhole.

7. Pull the threads to the wrong side of the fabric, tie in a knot and cut. Open the buttonhole with a seam ripper.

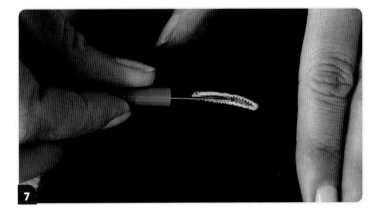

SNAPS

Snaps consist of two interlocking parts. They are quick to sew and very useful as closures because they do not require buttonholes.

1. Sew the female part by stitching in the side notches.

2. Stitch all four notches. Match the male part and sew in the same way.

TIP

Determine the location of the second part by passing a pin through the fabric and the tip of the female part, overlapping the two edges as before. At the pinning point, place two pins in a cross pattern.

HOOKS / HOOK-AND-LOOP TAPE / FROG CLOSURES

Here are three fastening systems that are less commonly used nowadays but are still very useful for clothing, bags, or costumes.

HOOKS (A)

Sew them well to the edge of the garment so the fastener does not show. Mark their position with pins or a few stitches before starting. Match the male part with the female part. Sew the hook to a double layer of fabric, buttonhole stitch, and do several stitches on top of each other to secure it.

HOOK-AND-LOOP TAPE (B)

It is composed of two self-gripping bands: a velvet part and a crochet (hook) part (hence the name Velcro). It is convenient for children's costumes.

Hook-and-loop tape is relatively solid and thick, so it is imperative to machine stitch. Cut two strips of hook-and-loop tape. Place and then pin the strips. Machine stitch.

FROG CLOSURES (C)

Place the two parts of the frog closure on each side. Lightly overlap the edges of the garment. There will be some movement in this closure.

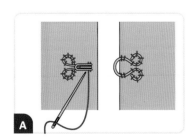

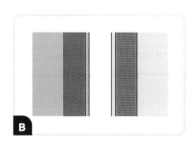

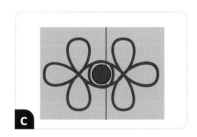

ZIPPERS

SEWING A ZIPPER BY HAND

Buy a zipper longer than you need; you can easily cut it to size when finished.

1. Cut the fabric neatly into a rectangle. Place the zipper, front sides together, on one edge. Stitch using a straight stitch on the zipper tape.

2. Open the zipper (this step will be helpful for further assembly, especially on zippered bags).

3. Place the second part of the zipper on the second edge, still front sides together. Stitch.

4. Overlap stitches at each end of the zipper. Trim the zipper with big scissors (not sewing scissors!).

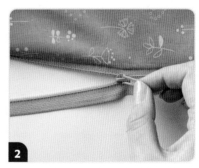

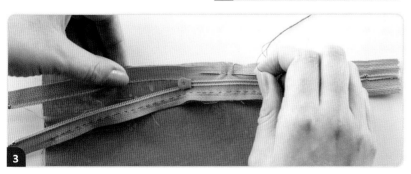

SEWING A SEPARATING ZIPPER BY MACHINE

Sewing machines are usually sold with various feet, including the special zipper foot. The zipper foot is split into two parts, allowing the needle to be positioned on either side of the zipper. There are different ways to assemble a zipper depending on the model and the garment's cut.

1. On each edge of a piece of fabric where the zipper will be inserted, fold over ⅜″ (1cm) to the back side. Press. Pin the zipper to one side. Baste.

2. Baste the other part of the zipper to the second side.

3. Change the presser foot. Install the special zipper presser foot. Position the needle to the right. Stitch the first side of the zipper.

4. Open the zipper and position the needle to the left. Stitch the second side.

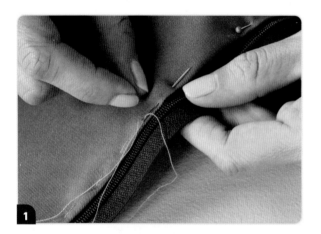

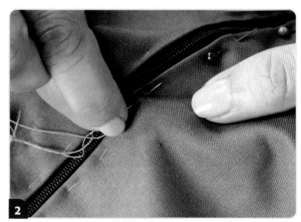

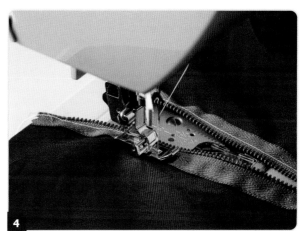

SEWING A NON-SEPARATING ZIPPER BY MACHINE

EXPOSED ZIPPER

This is a fashionable closure in which the zipper is a design detail.

1. Choose a pretty zipper. You can choose a fancy or contrasting color zipper. You can sew the zipper onto a prepared seam or you can add it to a solid piece of fabric by slitting the fabric the length of the zipper.

2. Overcast the edges if you cut a new slit for the zipper. Position the closed zipper. Baste the zipper in place.

3. Change the presser foot on the machine to a special zipper presser foot. Adjust the needle. Refer to your machine manual, as each model has its own setting.

4. Stitch the open zipper on both sides.

SEW A HIDDEN ZIPPER

Choose a zipper color that coordinates with the fabric.

1. Fold over ³⁄₁₆″ (0.5cm) to the back side on each side of the opening left for the zipper. Press to hold the fold in place.

2. Turn the garment front side out. Pin the closed zipper in the opening, aligning the top of the slider with the top of the garment. If you wish to add a hook and eye at the top , leave ³⁄₈″ (1cm) at the top of the garment.

3. Baste the zipper in place. It is not possible to machine stitch with pins.

4. Install a special zipper presser foot on the machine. Read the machine instructions, as you may need to change the needle position to stitch.

5. Machine stitch each side of the zipper, and move the needle. Stitch with the zipper open. When the presser foot reaches the zipper slider level, stop sewing, raise the presser foot, slide the slider to the other side of the presser foot, and resume sewing.

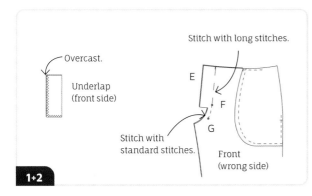

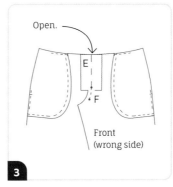

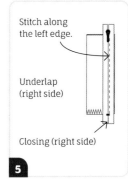

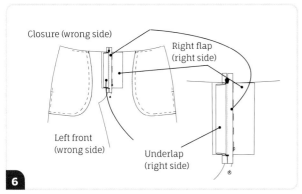

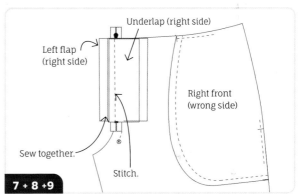

ASSEMBLING A FLY

This flap closure is placed on the front of a pair of pants, shorts, or skirt, in the seam where the legs meet. For men, the left side covers the right, and vice versa for women.

1. Fold the underlap wrong side together, and overcast the outer edges.

2. Position the fronts, right sides together:

▸ **a.** Stitch between E and F with maximum stitch length.

▸ **b.** Stitch between F and G with standard stitch length.

3. Open the flaps along the center front seam (EF).

4. Position the zipper on the underlap, right sides together, along the length.

5. Stitch along the left edge of the zipper with the zipper machine foot.

6. On the front's wrong side, position the zipper's free side along the center front (EF), right sides together, and pin the zipper and left flap.

7. Place the left front flap over the underlap, right sides together.

The zipper will be between the left flap and the underlap.

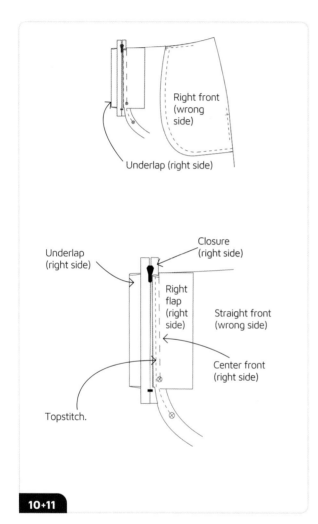

Right front (wrong side)

Underlap (right side)

Underlap (right side)

Closure (right side)

Right flap (right side)

Straight front (wrong side)

Center front (right side)

Topstitch.

10+11

8. Stitch the left flap, zipper, and underlap together flush with the zipper teeth.

9. Trim excess left flap flush with the underlap.

10. Fold the underlap, zipper, and left flap to the wrong side of the flap.

11. Topstitch ³⁄₁₆″ (5mm) from the zipper teeth.

12. Pin the underlap to the left front of the pants.

13. Pin the right flap, right sides together, to the right side of the zipper. Be careful not to pin the right front of the pants. Stitch flush with the zipper teeth.

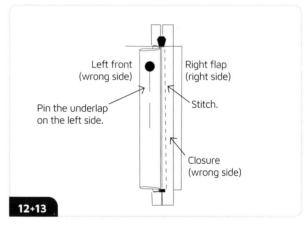

Left front (wrong side)

Right flap (right side)

Pin the underlap on the left side.

Stitch.

Closure (wrong side)

12+13

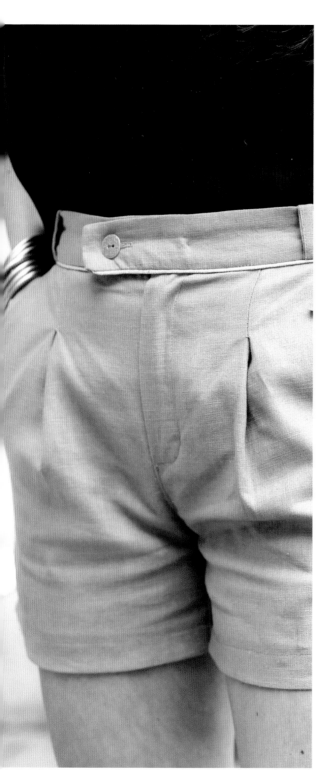

14. Pin the right flap and zipper to the right front of the pants, wrong sides together.

15. On the right side of the pants, draw a vertical line 1⅛″ (3cm) from the center front (EF) to ¾″ (2cm) from F and then an arc to F.

16. Stitch the vertical line.

17. Remove the pin holding the underlap on the left side and fold the underlap over to the right side. Stitch the round (so you are also stitching the underlap).

18. Undo the seam between E and F with a seam ripper.

19. Trim the excess zipper underneath point F.

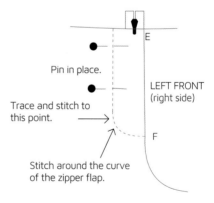

Pin in place.

Trace and stitch to this point.

Stitch around the curve of the zipper flap.

LEFT FRONT (right side)

ASSEMBLING A ZIPPER WITH A LINING

The zipper can be sewn between two fabrics.

1. Lay the zipper on the exterior fabric, right sides together and edge to edge. Pin. Place the start of the zipper as close to the neckline as possible. You can either fold the zipper tape over or cut it off.

2. Pull the lining over so that the lining and exterior fabric are right sides together. Pin everything together again: exterior fabric + zipper + lining. You will have to lower the zipper slider by about 4″ (10cm).

3. Change the sewing machine foot and install the zipper foot; be careful to clip it on the right side. Make your seam by aligning the edge of the fabrics with your ⅜″ (1cm) mark. Before reaching the zipper slider, insert the needle into the fabric and raise the presser foot. Slide your hand inside the material and gently move the slider up.

Lower the presser foot and finish your seam up to the notch. You will extend this notch to the stop point of your stitching.

4. Turn right side out and press. Be careful; the zipper prongs are plastic and can melt. Do not press too closely.

5. Repeat the steps above on the other side. Do not hesitate to lower the slider, and do not forget to change the side of the zipper foot. At the end of this seam, notch it to your stop point. Turn the work over through the opening left in the lining, tuck the lining into the garment, and press lightly.

EYELETS

Eyelets are an easy way to make a bag opening.

1. Mark the location of the eyelets with an erasable pen. Mark the point in the center of the grommet (take the grommet, place it on this point, and draw a line through the grommet).

2. Cut out the circle with the tip of your scissors.

3. Place the top part of the eyelet in the hole, then place the bottom part underneath.

4. Use the kit from the box and a hammer to close the eyelet.

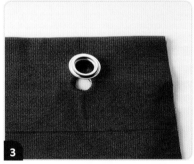

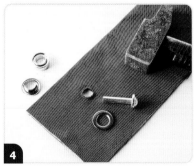

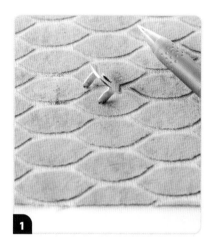

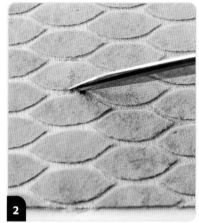

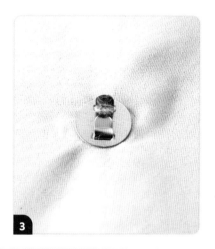

MAGNETS

APPLYING MAGNETIC SNAPS

Applying magnetic snaps makes it easy to close a bag.

1. Mark the location of the magnet on the front of the bag with an erasable pen.

2. Make a cut with the tip of your scissors (a tiny notch is enough) so that the prongs of the magnet can pass through the fabric.

3. Pass the prongs of the magnet through the notches and place the metal plate underneath to fold the prongs over.

4. Repeat with the other part of the magnet (male side) on each side of the flap.

INSTALLING AN INVISIBLE MAGNET

Installing an invisible magnet allows you to make a discreet bag closure.

1. Mark the location of the magnet on the back side of the lining, referring to the pattern.

2. Attach the magnet with glue or a small piece of double-sided tape.

3. With a zipper presser foot, stitch all the way around the magnet.

4. Proceed in the same way to place the other part of the magnet on the flap.

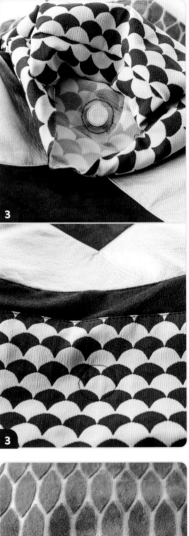

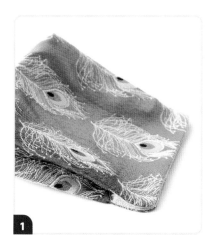

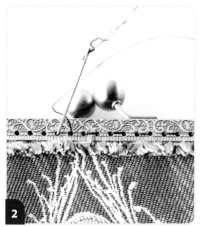

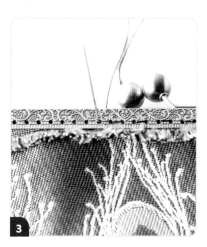

ATTACHING A CLASP

**Attaching an antique clasp
embellishes a small purse.**

1. Pre-form the fold on the side of the
bag along the long seam.

2. Thread a needle with a cording
thread and sew the clasp by inserting
the needle into the spaces provided.

3. Sew the clasp by passing the thread
over/under in all the spaces provided.

4. Repeat until you reach the last space,
then tie a secure knot.

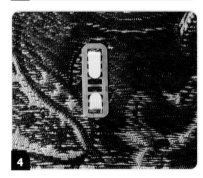

PURSE BUCKLES

The installation of purse buckles is based on the principle of the clasp.

1. Shape the fabric tabs, turn them over, and iron them. Mark the location of the top purse buckles on the flap and the front. Sew the tabs to the edge of the flap.

2. Place the purse buckle on the flap, taking in all the thicknesses; then tighten with jewelry pliers.

3. On the front of the purse, mark the location of the bottom buckle and make small notches with the tip of your scissors. Position the buckle in place.

4. Position the plate and fold down the prongs by hand or with pliers.

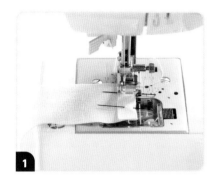

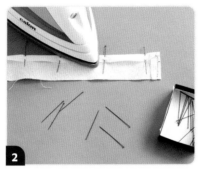

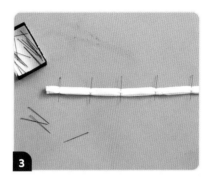

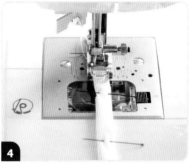

Very useful in sewing, bindings serve as a fastener and decoration.

1. Cut a rectangle to size. Fold over ³⁄₁₆″ (0.5cm) on the short sides and stitch.

2. Fold over ⅜″ (0.5cm) on the long sides. Pin, then press.

3. Fold the strip in half and pin.

4. Stitch along the entire length of the tie, ⅛″ (2mm) flush with the edge.

5. Pin the ties to the front side of one fabric, edge to edge; then place the second fabric on top. Stitch, sandwiching the ties between the fabrics, and turn right side out.

SEWING A BUTTON LOOP CLOSURE

Easy to sew, the loop is always placed at the edge of the fabric, raw edges hidden in a seam.

1. Measure the height of your chosen button and add 1⅝″ (4cm). Cut the fabric or cord you want to use as a loop according to this dimension.

2. Mark the center of the pouch and pin the loop on each side to the right side of the fabric. Lay the second fabric on top, right sides together.

3. Pin the entire length, then stitch, sandwiching the loop.

4. Press the seams open and turn the work right side out.

DECORATIONS

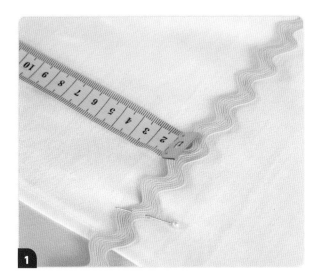

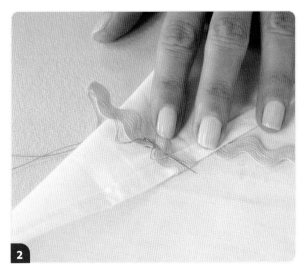

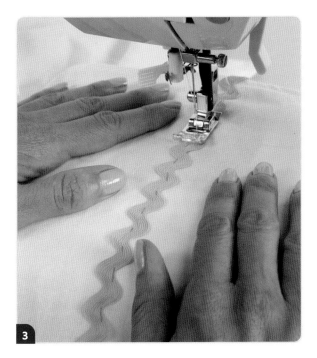

SEWING RICKRACK BRAID

Adding rickrack can lighten up a garment or decorative item. It can change the look and give a retro feel to your creations.

1. Choose the location of the rickrack, and measure and mark. Center the rickrack over the marks.

2. Pin the rickrack evenly. Baste.

3. Stitch in one seam down the middle of the rickrack.

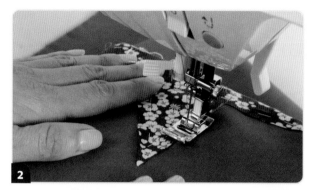

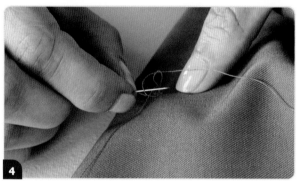

An appliqué can be used to personalize a cushion, bag, or garment.

1. Pin the design to the selected fabric on the right side.

2. Baste evenly ⅜″ (1cm) from the edge.

3. Set the sewing machine to a zigzag stitch. Set the stitch size to 1 or 2 (very tight). Stitch all around the design following the contours.

4. To turn, insert the needle, lift the presser foot, and rotate, following the pattern. Lower the presser foot and follow the pattern. Finish by tucking the threads to the back side.

TECHNIQUES // DECORATIONS

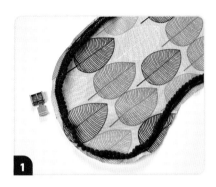
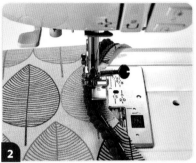
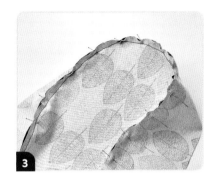

APPLY POM-POM TRIM

1. Change the foot of your sewing machine: Install the zipper foot, moving the needle to the left position. Use pins to position your pom-pom trim around the main piece on the right side. The pom-poms should be ⅜″ (1cm) from the edge of your fabric. Pin the trim in place. Feel free to use a lot of pins.

If you are more comfortable, baste the trim by hand before stitching it on the sewing machine.

2. Stitch ⅜″ (1cm) from the edge. Your needle will come as close to the pom-poms as possible. Bring the ends of the pop-pom trim together by overlapping them.

3. Place the second piece of fabric on top of the main piece, right sides together, and pin around.

4. Place the work under the sewing machine. Keeping the same foot, join the fabrics by stitching back into the assembly stitching of the pompom braid.

5. Once the pompom braid is installed; put the standard foot back on your sewing machine.

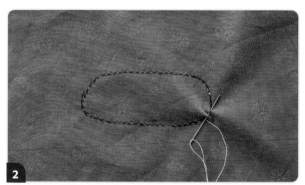

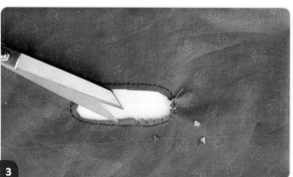

HANDLES

SEWING A HANDLE OPENING INTO THE BODY OF THE BAG

This type of handle will allow you to create bags and pouches using only fabric.

1. For each bag side, layer two fabrics right sides together. Mark the location of the handle.

2. Sew the two layers using a straight stitch and following the line.

3. Cut open the handle area with scissors and notch evenly.

4. Turn the fabrics over through the handle.

5. Place both sides of the bag front sides together and stitch on three sides.

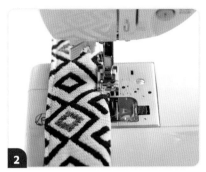

MAKING A HANDLE

For a handle to be sturdy and have staying power, it must be topstitched and padded. This also gives it a nice look.

1. Stitch the two handle strips together lengthwise, right sides together. Fold the top and bottom hems with an iron. Place the interfacing strip on the top or bottom of the handle on the wrong side of the fabric.

2. Fold the strip in half, wrong sides together, and pin the inside hem. Stitch ⅛″ (3mm) from the edge on each side.

3. Draw four lines ⅜″ (1cm) apart with a ruler.

4. Stitch on all four lines.

5. Pin the handle to its support and stitch.

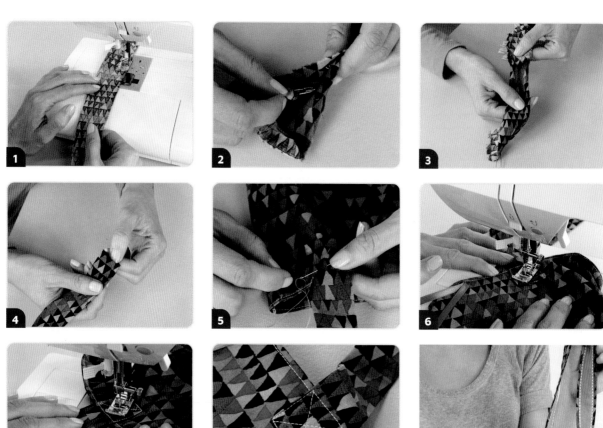

SEWING A HANDLE

Knowing how to add handles and strengthen them with cross-stitching will allow you to sew durable bags.

1. Fold a strip of fabric in half, right sides together. Stitch.

2. Fix a safety pin to one end.

3. Turn the handle right side out with the safety pin.

4. Tuck the ends of the handles inside.

5. Place the handles on top of their support, 1⅝″ (4cm) from the edge. Baste.

6. Stitch into a square shape. Stitch a diagonal in this square.

7. Stitch the other diagonal.

8. Stitch into the square in the shape of a cross.

MAKE A LOOP HANDLE

This decorative element borrowed from ready-made accessories offers a refined finish. The double straight stitching plays up the originality with contrasting colors.

1. Fold over the end of a long strip ⅜″, wrong sides together, and stitch the end with a ³⁄₁₆″ (0.5cm) hem.

2. Fold over ⅜″ (1cm) on one side of each of the long and short strips, wrong side together. Fold each strip in half, wrong sides together, and stitch ⅛″ (3mm) from the edges.

3. Fold the large and small strips through either side of a ring and pin.

4. Attach the handle by hand.

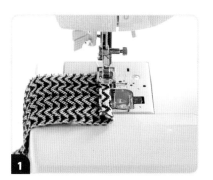

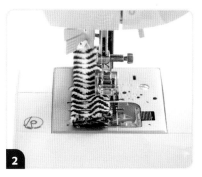

TIPS & TRICKS

HERE ARE SOME TIPS TO NEVER GET STUCK IN THE MIDDLE OF A PROJECT!

PROBLEMS WITH THREADING THE SEWING MACHINE

I CAN'T GET THE THREAD TO COME UP FROM THE BOBBIN; WHY?

Hold the bobbin thread while turning the handwheel to lower the needle and the thread that will catch the bobbin thread.

Then using a flat instrument (a ruler or a pair of scissors), grab the loop formed under the presser foot and slide it to the side.

I THREADED THE THREAD ON MY MACHINE, BUT IT DOESN'T WANT TO SEW; IT SEEMS STUCK.

First, check that the bobbin winding lever some machines have in the bobbin area has not accidentally shifted into the position to make a bobbin (stopping the machine from stitching).

Then check that the bobbin is installed correctly. Remember that the bobbin must be placed in the bobbin case with the thread winding counterclockwise (unless otherwise stated in your machine manual).

THE BOBBIN THREAD BREAKS.

▸ The bobbin is incorrectly threaded and must be re-threaded.

▸ The bobbin case is dirty. It must be cleaned by removing all the dust.

THE UPPER THREAD BREAKS.

Repeat the overall threading and change the needle, ensuring the needle and thread are compatible. If it doesn't work, adjust the tension.

MY BOTTOM STITCH DOESN'T LOOK GOOD; IT'S MAKING LOOPS.

Check that:

▸ The presser foot is down. We often forget to lower the presser foot at the beginning of our sewing. If the foot is not lowered, it cannot press properly on the fabric, and the feed dogs will not be able to move the fabric forward properly.

▸ The bobbin is evenly and smoothly wound. If the thread is loose on the bobbin, wind a new one.

Correct

To be redone

▶ The threads are identical in the spool and bobbin. Often, when the threads are of different quality, the tensions on the threads are different.

▶ The bobbin case is correctly tensioned (and not holding the bobbin thread too tightly). If the bobbin case is too tight, loosen it slightly to regulate the bobbin tension. For vertically mounted bobbins (accessed under the machine bed at either the front or side) remove the bobbin case and adjust the tension by turning the little screw in the bobbin case very slightly. For horizontal bobbin holders (those mounted in the top of the machine bed just in front of the presser foot) unscrew the machine plate, remove the bobbin case and again loosen the screw (turn to the left) or tighten it (turn to the right). Feel the tension of the thread as it exits the bobbin case. Fine-tuning bobbing tension by turning this screw will help your stitches become nice and even again.

▶ The tension of the bobbin thread has not moved (between 4 and 6, depending on the machine) on the knob of the machine. If the spool thread pulls too much or gets trapped, try loosening the knob by turning it to a lower number.If the thread does not pull tight, the ten-sion is too low, and turn it to a higher number. Moving the tension adjustment knob is the first step. If this doesn't help, try cleaning between the two discs with a business card.

MY TOP THREAD KEEPS BREAKING!

Check that:

▶ The spool thread is properly threaded. This is often the first cause of thread breakage. The easiest way is to undo it all and start over. This is the fastest way. Once the thread is rethreaded, everything should be fine.

If not, check that the threads are identical on the spool and bobbin. Are they the same thickness and quality?

▶ The bobbin holder is not too tight and the thread does not struggle to come out. If it does, loosen it.

▶ The tension selector has not moved and does not indicate too high a tension.

▶ The needle is not blunt, bent, or not suitable for the fabric selected. If it is, change the needle. The hook, bobbin case, or needle plate may have rough edges that catch and break the thread.

WHEN AND HOW SHOULD I ADJUST THE THREAD TENSION?

Tension is usually set between 4 and 6, depending on the machine. When you sew for the first time, check your stitches: If they look good on top and underneath, the tension is correct. The thread should slide easily off the spool, and the metal discs should not be too tight.

It will be necessary to change the tension if the stitches are not nice and even, or when you need to change the thickness of the thread, such as extra strong thread for topstitching denim or a fragile thread such as silk thread.

You will need to lower the thread tension if you are sewing jersey or knit fabrics and stitching stretches and waves the fabrics, or when sewing a hem with a twin needle and you see a ridge between the two lines of stitching.

PROBLEMS WHEN SEWING

MY MACHINE IS VERY NOISY.

The hook or needle bar is not properly greased. They need to be lubricated with a few drops of sewing machine oil. This is usually supplied with the machine.

The needle is dull or bent. Simply replace it with a new needle.

I CAN'T START MY SEAM.

The presser foot is tilted because the fabric is thick.

▸ Take a piece of fabric and fold it to be the same thickness as the fabric to be sewn.

▸ Place it halfway under your presser foot before your needle, stuck to your fabric and ready to sew.

▸ The feed dogs can move forward and push this fabric "shim" toward the back of the machine. It will not be sewn.

MY SEAMS ARE UNEVEN.

There can be several reasons for uneven seams:

▸ You need to adjust the thread tension (start with the bobbin case).

▸ The bobbin case can also be dirty. It should be cleaned in case lint is causing the bobbin from turning freely.

THE MACHINE SKIPS STITCHES.

▸ The needle you are sewing with is unsuitable for the fabric you are using. This often happens when trying to sew elastic fabrics with standard needles.

▸ The needle is blunt or bent (which can be seen quite easily by turning it between your fingers or putting it on a table). If this is the case, it must be changed. It is vital to change the needle regularly (or there is a risk of damaging the machine and the fabric).

▸ The hook (at the level of the needle) is perhaps shifted. You must check it by removing the needle.

If this works, the hook is out of place, and the machine should be sent for service.

Unfortunately, the needles may be simply of poor quality. As for the thread, it is better to prioritize quality, even if it is a little more expensive, to make quality garments.

It is essential to use bobbins compatible with the machine. A few millimeters, more or less, can make a difference.

In any case, before making any adjustments to the machine, remember to put in a new needle.

THE THREADS GET TANGLED

▸ If the bobbin is improperly filled, the needle encounters several threads that eventually form knots. Carefully cut the threads, remove the bobbin, empty it, and replace the thread. Knots can also be caused by a loose presser foot. In this case, tighten it with a screwdriver.

WHEN I FINISH SEWING AND WANT TO REMOVE MY FABRIC, I CAN'T. IT JAMS, OR AT LEAST THREE THREADS ARE COMING OUT …

▸ The sewing machine has not finished its stitch. The machine stitch is made between the needle thread and the bobbin thread. The thread will get stuck if the needle has not finished coming up.

Hold the fabric with your left hand while pulling slightly to the side. Simultaneously with your right hand, turn the handwheel (on the right side of the machine) towards you to move the needle down and then up.

▸ The fabric will become easy to pull, and there will be only two threads left: one from the spool and one from the bobbin.

WHY DOES MY NEEDLE BREAK?

▸ The needle is twisted and caught by the hook.

▸ The needle is twisted by the bobbin, which is poorly positioned, and drags it.

▸ The needle has been chosen incorrectly and is too thin for the thickness of the fabric to be sewn.

▸ The needle is too thin for the thickness of the thread.

▸ This also happens if we push our fabric a little too hard.

▸ The needle quickly passes over the pins placed vertically on the fabric, but sometimes, with speed, it can hit one of them and break.

THE FABRIC WRINKLES OR GETS TRAPPED

▸ The fabric feed is defective. The feed dogs should be checked and cleaned if necessary.

▸ The foot pressure may need to be adjusted.

▸ The fabric is too thin for the machine; a stabilizer should be placed underneath the fabric.

I CAN'T SEW MY FABRIC.

▶ When sewing thick fabrics (e.g., fleece), you may have difficulty starting the seam or topstitching in the corners, for example. This is because the material tends to "skate," and the needle always pricks in the same place.

▶ Place a piece of tissue or parchment paper between the fabric and the sewing machine's feed dogs.

HOW DO I USE A CONE WITH MY SEWING MACHINE?

For sewing, we usually use spools of thread. But you can also use thread cones.

It is not possible to put them directly on your machine, but you have several solutions:

▶ Buy a cone holder and place it on top before you start threading through your machine. This is the ideal solution.

▶ Use a heavy enough cup or can on your sewing table and place the cone inside. That will help keep the cone stationary. Position it so that the thread is taut.

I'M NOT HAPPY WITH MY SEWING, OR I'VE CAUGHT ANOTHER FABRIC (USING THE SEAM RIPPER QUICKLY).

You've just sewn together fabrics, and you're disappointed when you check your seam. The stitches are not well done, the fabric has moved, or you have caught a piece of cloth from another part of your creation.

Don't panic. Use a seam ripper to undo the poorly made stitches.

Once the stitches are undone, don't hesitate to iron your fabrics again and re-pin them. There's no need to sew the whole length if part of your seam is fine.

Restitch the seam a few stitches (3–4 stitches) before the space to be sewn and 3–4 stitches after unless you are finishing your seam at the end of the fabric. In this case, reverse as you usually do.

WHAT IF I RUN OUT OF THREAD IN THE MIDDLE OF A SEAM?

We often run out of the bobbin (and sometimes the spool) in the middle of a seam.

Don't worry; you don't have to undo and redo the seam from the beginning. Pick up the seam a few stitches before the last one ends, then continue as normal.

`TIPS`

HOW DO I MAKE SURE I DON'T GO TOO FAR WHEN SEWING THE STITCHES OF A BUTTONHOLE?

Slip a pin across the end of the buttonhole. This will prevent you from stitching too far when you see the end of the buttonhole.

HOW TO SEW BUTTONS IN A STRAIGHT LINE?

Here's a reliable technique:

▸ Mark the location of your buttons (tailor's chalk, chalk pencil, or pencil).

▸ Attach the buttons to the marks with clear tape.

▸ Sew, then remove the tape. Your buttons will be perfectly sewn.

IF YOU HAVE WORN PINS THAT DON'T SLIDE AS WELL ...

Stick them in a bar of soap. You will then be able to stick them quickly into the fabric.

HOW TO MAKE REGULAR SPACES WHEN HAND-STITCHING?

▸ Draw 2 lines with the desired gap on the thumb of the hand you are not sewing with (the left hand, for example).

▸ Hold the fabric to be sewn with that hand, shifting your thumb at each stitch you sew.

MIRROR CUTTING

If it is impossible to fold the fabric in half, remember to turn the pattern over to cut the second side so that you have a right and left piece each time.

SPEED

▸ Stitch at a uniform speed to ensure even stitches.

STITCH TEST

▸ Before starting a project, always do a trial run to avoid problems and determine the proper stitch length and width.

IF YOU DO NOT HAVE A SERGER

▸ **When joining stretchy fabrics,** set your machine to a stretch stitch. The symbol for this might look like a slanted zigzag. This stitch is sometimes therefore called a "lightening stitch." If your machine does not have this, adjust to a narrow zigzag stitch that it is both tight enough not to show on the right side of the garment and wide enough to work with the elasticity of the fabric. To find the right setting, test the fabric scraps left from cutting out your pieces.

▸ **For classic overlocking on a sewing machine,** set your machine to an overlock stitch (check your sewing machine manual) and try to position the swing of the stitch to land close to the raw edge of the fabric to be seamed.

GLOSSARY

A

▶ **Applique:** A fabric shape that is sewn onto another fabric with a satin stitch (very tight zigzag). This shape can be reinforced with iron-on web. It is a decorative element.

▶ **Armhole:** Opening of a garment to which the sleeves are fitted.

B

▶ **Backstitch:** Backstitches are made at the beginning and end of each seam on the machine to secure the thread.

▶ **Basting:** Sewing temporarily, by hand or machine, to hold pieces together before sewing them permanently. Large stitches are usually used.

▶ **Basting thread:** A flexible, non-marking thread that breaks easily and is ideal for temporary sewing.

▶ **Bias-bound seam:** Finishing a raw seam edge with bias tape.

▶ **Bias cut:** Cut at 45° to the weft thread.

▶ **Binding:** Finishing raw edges with a strip of fabric such as bias tape, braid trim, or lace to prevent the material from fraying.

▶ **Bobbin:** Small plastic or metal spool located in the base of the sewing machine below the presser foot. It supplies the lower thread that forms the underside of the stitch, with the upper thread fed by the spool on the top of the machine forming the upper side of the stitch.

▸ **Buttonhole:** The hole that a button passes through, often sewn with a specific foot on a sewing machine.

▸ **Buttonloop:** A small loop of braided thread for a button to pass through, typically used for garment closures.

▸ **Button placket:** The double layers of fabric that hold the buttons and button-holes in a shirt.

C

▸ **Column:** Each knitted fabric consists of columns of stitches that run vertically and correspond to the overlapping of stitches.

▸ **Cone:** Serger thread is most often sold on thread cones. There are many colors and materials.

▸ **Crotch:** Seam in the middle of the front and back of a pair of pants.

▸ **Cutting Line:** A line printed on the pattern as a guide for cutting. A multiple-size pattern has several cutting lines.

▸ **Cutting plan:** A drawing showing how to lay the pattern pieces on the fabric to optimize the amount of fabric.

D

▸ **Dart:** A triangular-shaped fold that adjusts a garment to the body's curves.

▸ **Double hem:** A double-folded, topstitched finish.

E

▸ **Ease:** The slight fullness of one piece of clothing in relation to another to which it is to be joined. The ease is calculated to give comfort.

▸ **Easing In:** A machine stitch that eases fabric into a seam (such as the waistline of a garment).

▸ **To ease:** In Construction to shape a slightly larger volume of fabric to fit a smaller edge to build in shape, as in easing in the top of a sleeve cap so it fits into a sleeve.

▸ **Wearing ease:** The extra fabric added to body measurements in a garment to allow for comfortable movement.

F

▸ **Facing:** A piece of fabric lining the edge of a neckline, waistline, pocket opening to give it a clean and neat finish.

▸ **Flat fell seam:** A sturdy, firm seam, often used in jeans, in which the the seam allowances are turned under and top-stitched to the right side of the garment. To construct, the seam is first sewn right sides together, then one seam allowance is trimmed, and finally the remaining, longer, seam allowance is pressed under and topstitched down to cover it.

▸ **French seam:** Often used to sew light or transparent fabric. This seam is sewn twice, once, wrong sides together, and then again right sides together, to contain all raw edges in a neat fold.

▸ **Fold line:** Is used to indicate where the fabric should be folded. Half pattern pieces are often instructed to be laid along the fold line so when the fabric is unfolded a complete pattern piece has been cut.

▸ **Frog closure:** A decorative fastener made with a soutache or a cord arranged in four overlapping loops secured at the center. The matching button is made with the same cord in a special knot.

G

▶ **Gathering stitching:** Sew two rows of long hand or machine stitches along a fabric edge. The threads are then tied at the end and pulled to gather evenly to fit a smaller piece of fabric. Tulle is usually gathered by hand.

▶ **Grosgrain:** A fabric ribbon with distinctive ridges, sold by the yard or meter.

▶ **Guideline:** Tiny grooves placed on the needle plate and parallel to the presser foot as guides for sewing straight seams.

▶ **Gusset:** A small piece of fabric placed in a slit or seam to provide additional ease.

H

▶ **Hemming:** Finishing the bottom of a sleeve, dress, skirt, pants, etc. by folding the edge to the inside of the garment and attaching by hand or machine. A twin-needle hem, stitched from the right side with a double needle, is one option.

▶ **Hem allowance:** The measurement of the folded hem depth.

I

▶ **Iron-on:** This is a type of iron-on interfacing with heat-sensitive glue on one side. Used to add structure and to reinforce fabric.

▶ **Interfacing:** Used under the main fabric to stiffen (collar, shirt cuffs), give support (strapless, close-fitting garments), or to reinforce (areas subject to repeated stress: shirt buttonholes, coat). Interfacing can be attached to the garment fabric either by fusing with an iron, or sewn-in.

J

▶ **Joining:** Stitching two or more fabrics together on a sewing machine.

L

▶ **Lining:** A second layer of fabric sewn to the inside of the garment as a final finish

M

▶ **Mirror cut:** When one piece must be cut in one direction, and the other must be cut in the opposite direction, in vertical symmetry.

▶ **Mitered Corner:** A distinctive diagonal seam formed when the fabric is folded to go around a corner (hems meeting at the bottom of a sleeve slit or curtain, for example).

▶ **Multiple-size pattern:** Pattern with different cutting lines for each size printed on it.

▶ **Muslin:** A test version of a garment made in inexpensive fabric to check the fit and fall of the garment before sewing it in the final fabric.

N

▶ **Needle plate:** A small metal plate on the bed of the machine under the presser foot. It usually has tiny grooves parallel to the presser foot as guides for accurate stitching of straight seams, A hole in the center allows the needle to connect with the bobbin thread and make a stitch.

▸ **Neckline:** Part of a garment that surrounds the neck.

▸ **Notch:** A reference point for garment assembly.

▸ **Notching:** Use the tip of the scissors to make small simple or V-shaped cuts on the edge of the fabric within the seam allowances. These notches reduce bulk along the seams when they are turned right side out. This is usually done for curved seamlines (concave or convex).

O

▸ **On the fold:** Often referred to in pattern layout when a half garment pattern piece is laid "on the fold" so when the fabric is unfolded a complete pattern piece has been cut.

▸ **Open seam:** When pressing, spread the seam allowances open with the iron to flatten them on both sides of the seam. This allows the seam to be as flat as possible.

▸ **Overcasting:** Using a zigzag stitch sew close to the cut edge of fabric. This prevents the fabric from fraying and unraveling the seam itself.

▸ **Overlay:** A second pattern piece that is layered over another garment piece.

▸ **Overstitching:** Sewing stitches on the right side of the fabric parallel to the assembly seam (about ¼″ or 5 or 6mm). This gives a clean and decorative finish.

P

▸ **Pattern markings:** Symbols printed on the pattern as construction information such as notches used to match pattern pieces, fold line, and placement for buttonholes etc.

▸ **Pinning:** Place two pieces of fabric right sides together and edges aligned, then stick your pins perpendicular to the edge of the fabric (before going to a fitting or sewing).

▸ **Piping:** A covered cord used as a decorative detail along edges. Made of the cord wrapped with fabric and the narrow strip of flat fabric that is sewn into the seam.

▸ **Pivot:** Stop the machine with the needle still in the fabric, then lift the presser foot turn the fabric and continue stitching.

▸ **Pocket bag:** Hidden inside of a pocket remaining on the back of the garment.

▸ **Presser foot:** The flat metal piece at the end of the shank of the needle bar that must be lowered onto the fabric to hold it flat for stitching.

▸ **Pressing sheet:** A piece of fabric generally in cotton that is placed on a more fragile fabric (wool, silk ...) during ironing.

R

▸ **Raw edge:** Unfinished fabric edge, which frays.

▸ **Reinforce:** To strengthen a heavily-worn or stressed part of a garment (such as a buttonhole) with rows of extra stitching or a piece of fabric.

▸ **Ribbing:** Elastic fabric found on the edges of jackets, sweatshirts, etc.

▸ **Right Side:** The side of the fabric that appears on the outside of the finished garment (the side where the pattern is visible when there is one). When pinning or sewing pattern pieces, the fabric is often positioned right sides together.

▶ **Right sides together:** This term is used a lot in sewing instructions. It means that the fabrics to be sewn are placed one on top of the other, with the printed side of one facing the printed side of the other. Thus, the seam is on the wrong side when you turn the fabrics over after sewing.

▶ **Rolled:** A small, skinny hem at the edge of the fabric, held in place by the side stitches.

▶ **Row:** Each knitted fabric consists of rows of stitches that run horizontally and are made up of the succession of stitches produced.

S

▶ **Selvage:** The edge of a fabric that doesn't fray, parallel to the warp threads.

▶ **Selvage to selvage:** Taking the left side of the fabric and folding it over to the right side.

▶ **Seam allowance:** The amount of fabric set aside along a line of stitching to join two parts.

▶ **Seamline:** The actual stitching line of the seam.

▶ **Seams included:** Some patterns take into account the width of the seam allowances in the pattern dimensions.

▶ **Seams not included:** When using patterns that do not consider the seam allowances, you must add the seam allowances before cutting the fabric. You will also need to add more length for hems.

▶ **Seam ripper:** A small sharp tool used to undo stitches made with the sewing machine, cutting the thread without cutting the fabric. It can also be used to open buttonholes.

▶ **Serger:** A machine that sews, overcasts, and cuts fabric in a single pass.

▶ **Sleeve board:** Mini ironing board used for seams and narrow parts of a garment.

▶ **Sleeve cap:** The upper part of the sleeve that joins the armhole at the shoulder seam. At the time of the assembly, one generally starts to pin the middle of the cap of the sleeve to the shoulder seam, then the edges of the bottom of the sleeve at the beginning of the side seam. Finally, any fullness at the sleeve cap is distributed by invisible gathers.

▶ **Smocking:** Decorative embroidery stitches made on the folds of a previously gathered fabric.

▶ **Spool:** Small cylinder on which thread is wound.

▶ **Stay stitching:** A row of stitches made in the seam allowance to prevent the fabric pieces from distorting, especially around necklines and armholes.

▶ **Stitch:** To assemble with the sewing machine.

▶ **Stitching guide:** An accessory that can be added to the machine at the needle plate to ensure straight seams.

▶ **Stitch length:** On a sewing machine, the distance between the two holes results from the needle passing through the fabric. The lower the number, the shorter the stitch. In general, shorter stitches are suitable for light fabrics, and longer stitches are preferable for heavy fabrics.

▶ **Stitch width:** On a sewing machine, represents the lateral movement of the needle from left to right. The straight stitch has a zero width.

T

▶ **Tailor's cushion or ham:** An accessory to simplify ironing. It has several curves and fabric can be placed over it during pressing to avoid creases.

▶ **Tension:** Pressure exerted on the thread. There are two tensions, one for the top thread and one for the bobbin thread. They should be set so that the stitch is neither loose nor tight.

▶ **Thread tension:** Part of the sewing machine settings. It is, in fact, unusual to modify it; it generally remains in the middle of the tension number range.

▶ **Top stitching:** A seam close to the edge to reinforce curved or slanted edges of pieces.

U

▶ **Under-stitching:** Stitching on the underside very close to an edge or seam. This allows the lining to be held in place.

W

▶ **Warp:** The vertical threads of the fabric parallel to the selvages, also known as straight of grain. The vertical grain, or threads are indicated on the pattern by an arrow. This arrow is used to orient the placement of the pieces on the fabric. Pull the fabric in both directions if you have a fabric without selvages. The straight of grain is in the direction where the fabric stretches the least.

▶ **Weft:** In a piece of woven fabric, the weft threads are perpendicular to the warp. They are slightly stretchy.

▶ **Width:** Width of the fabric, from selvage to selvage.

▶ **Wrong side of the fabric:** The side that appears on the inside of the finished garment (plain side of the printed fabric). The pattern pieces may be traced on the wrong side of the fabric.

▶ **Wrong sides together:** Place two pieces of fabric, one on top of the other, the back of one against the back of the other. The stitching will then show on the right side.

Y

▶ **Yoke:** Garment piece sewn to, or on top, of another pattern piece.

Z

▶ **Zigzag:** A sewing machine stitch that is useful for stretchy fabrics or overcasting the fabric's edge.

INDEX

METRIC CONVERSIONS

The metric measurements in this book follow standard conversion practices for sewing and soft crafts. The metric equivalents are often rounded off for ease of use. If you need more exact measurements, there are a number of amazing online converters.

The Complete Manual of Sewing

First published in the United States in 2022 by Stash Books, an imprint of C&T Publishing, Inc., P.O. Box 1456, Lafayette, CA 94549

Le manuel complet de la couture facile © 2020 by Éditions Marie Claire—Société d'Information et de Créations (SIC)

This edition of "*Le manuel complet de la couture facile*" first published in France by Éditions Marie Claire in 2020 is published by arrangement with Marie Claire.

PUBLISHER: Amy Barrett-Daffin

CREATIVE DIRECTOR: Gailen Runge

ACQUISITIONS EDITOR: Roxane Cerda

EDITOR: Jennifer Warren

ENGLISH-LANGUAGE COVER DESIGNER: April Mostek

ENGLISH TRANSLATION: Catherine Mourin

PRODUCTION COORDINATORS: Tim Manibusan and Zinnia Heinzmann

Attention Teachers: C&T Publishing, Inc., encourages the use of our books as texts for teaching. You can find lesson plans for many of our titles at ctpub.com or contact us at ctinfo@ctpub.com.

We take great care to ensure that the information included in our products is accurate and presented in good faith, but no warranty is provided, nor are results guaranteed. Having no control over the choices of materials or procedures used, neither the author nor C&T Publishing, Inc., shall have any liability to any person or entity with respect to any loss or damage caused directly or indirectly by the information contained in this book. For your convenience, we post an up-to-date listing of corrections on our website (ctpub.com). If a correction is not already noted, please contact our customer service department at ctinfo@ctpub.com or P.O. Box 1456, Lafayette, CA 94549.

Trademark (™) and registered trademark (®) names are used throughout this book. Rather than use the symbols with every occurrence of a trademark or registered trademark name, we are using the names only in the editorial fashion and to the benefit of the owner, with no intention of infringement.

Printed in China

10 9 8 7 6 5 4 3 2 1